The Making Of A Prophet

Timothy Long

Copyright © 2025 by Timothy Long

All rights reserved. No part of this publication may be reproduced, distributed or transmitted in any form or by any means, including photocopying, recording, or other electronic or mechanical methods, without the prior written permission of the publisher, except in the case of brief quotations embodied in critical reviews and certain other noncommercial uses permitted by copyright law. For mission requests, write to the publisher, addressed " Attention: Permissions Coordinator," at the address below.

Timothy Long/Rejoice Essential Publishing
PO BOX 512
Effingham, SC 29541
www.republishing.org

Unless otherwise indicated, scripture is taken from the King James Version.

The Holy Bible, English Standard Version (ESV) is adapted from the Revised Standard Version of the Bible, copyright Division of Christian Education of the National Council of the Churches of Christ in the U.S.A. All rights reserved.

Scripture quotations marked (NIV) are taken from the Holy Bible, New International Version®, NIV®. Copyright © 1973, 1978, 1984, 2011 by Biblica, Inc.™ Used by permission of Zondervan. All rights reserved worldwide. www.zondervan.com The "NIV" and "New International Version" are trademarks registered in the United States Patent and Trademark Office by Biblica, Inc.™

Scripture taken from the New King James Version®. Copyright © 1982 by Thomas Nelson. Used by permission. All rights reserved.

The Making Of A Prophet/Timothy Long

ISBN-13: 979-8-3492-3009-7

Preface

Greetings in the name of our Lord and Savior, Jesus Christ.

It is with immense joy and gratitude that I welcome you to the pages of "*The Making of a Prophet.*" As I pen down these words, my heart overflows with thanksgiving for the incredible journey that has brought us to this moment. I am Prophet Timothy Long, and it is both an honor and a privilege to share insights into the profound and transformative process of becoming a prophet. This book is not a mere guide for those with a prophetic calling; it is a beacon for all believers in Christ who hunger for a deeper understanding of the prophetic and a desire to grow in their spiritual walk with the Lord Jesus Christ.

In the intricate tapestry of my own journey, I have witnessed the unfathomable grace of our Lord Jesus Christ. From the moment He rescued me from the depths of darkness to the day He called me into the prophetic ministry, His hand has been the guiding force shaping my every step.

I extend my deepest gratitude to my loving wife, my seven children, and the wonderful church family at Jesus Christ for All Nations Church. Their unwavering support, prayers, and encouragement have been the wind beneath my wings. To my precious wife, your steadfast love has been my anchor, and I am profoundly grateful for your partnership in this incredible journey.

As we embark on this exploration of the making of a prophet, let it be known that the wisdom contained within these pages is not confined to a select few. It is an invitation for believers from all walks of life to glean from the rich insights of the prophetic journey. Whether you are a seasoned prophet, a burgeoning disciple, or someone seeking to understand the prophetic dynamics in the Kingdom of God, this book is for you.

I acknowledge the collective efforts of the Body of Christ, as we together seek the deeper mysteries of God. It is my prayer that this book serves as a roadmap, guiding you through the nuances of the prophetic calling and inspiring you to embrace the transformative work of the Holy Spirit in your life.

Above all, my gratitude extends to the Lord Jesus Christ, the Author, and Finisher of our faith. It is by His grace that I stand as a witness to His redemptive power, and it is through His Spirit that the prophetic calling has been kindled within me. To Him be all glory, honor, and praise.

May the words penned in these pages be a source of enlightenment, encouragement, and empowerment for your journey in the making of a prophet. Continue to pray and worship the Lord, and the possibilities are endless.

YOURS TRULY,
Prophet Timothy Long

Table of Contents

CHAPTER 1: The Prophetic Call Unveiled..................1
- Understanding the Purpose of God's Call to Prophetic Ministry.........1
- Unveiling God's Heart..................1
- Guiding and Correcting..................2
- Declaring God's Intentions..................2
- Bringing Comfort and Hope..................2
- Calling to Repentance and Transformation..................2
- Establishing Covenant Relationships..................3
- Anticipating Future Events..................3
- Demonstrating God's Faithfulness..................3
- The Whisper in the Silence..................4
- Navigating the Stirrings..................4
- The Uniqueness of Each Call..................5
- Embracing the Weight of the Call..................5
- Transparency in the Journey..................5
- Abraham: The Call to a New Land (Genesis 12:1-3)..................6
- Moses: The Burning Bush Encounter (Exodus 3:1-10)..................7
- Isaiah: The Vision in the Temple (Isaiah 6:1-8)..................7
- My Vision: The Burning Eagle and the Voice of Jesus..................7
- Understanding the Divine Call..................8
- Understanding the Source of Opposition..................9
- Scriptural Anchors for Resilience..................9
- Strategies for Overcoming Attacks..................9
- Perseverance as a Virtue..................10

CHAPTER 2: The Bedrock of Revelation: Building a Solid Spiritual

Foundation in the Word of God for Ministry..13
- The Word as a Source of Revelation..13
- Building Discernment through Scripture..14
- Scripture as a Mirror..14
- Prayerful Meditation on Scripture..14
- Navigating the Prophetic Path with Scripture.................................15
- Equipping Others with the Word..15
- A Prophetic Legacy Built on the Word...15
- Crafting and Upholding a Godly Identity in Prophetic Ministry.......16
- The Crucible of Character..16
- Personal Temptations and Triumphs..16
- Scriptural Wisdom on Character:..17
- Balancing Visibility and Humility..17
- A Legacy of Godly Character..18
- Prioritizing the Fruit of the Spirit over the Gifts in Prophetic Ministry.18
- The Distinction Between Gifts and Fruit..18
- Scriptural Foundations...19
- The Transient Nature of Gifts..19
- Fruit as the Sustaining Force..20
- Character as a Magnet for the Anointing...20
- Building a Lasting Legacy...20
- A Symphony of Fruit and Gifts..20

CHAPTER 3: Recognizing the Voice of God...22
- Creating Space for Divine Dialogue..22
- Biblical Anchors for Recognition..23
- Distinguishing God's Voice from Others...23
- The Language of Love...23
- Testing the Alignment with Scripture...24
- Personal Experiences and Lessons..24

- Practical Steps for Recognition..24
- The Symphony of Divine Communication.............................25
- Cultivating a Lifestyle of Sensitivity.......................................25
- Biblical Insights into Hearing God..25
- Embracing Visions and Dreams..26
- Hearing the Audible Voice..26
- Learning from Mistakes...26
- Tips for Growth...27
- The Symphony of God's Voice..27
- The Art of Discernment: Sharpening Your Prophetic Sensitivity for Accuracy..28
- Understanding the Essence of Discernment...........................28
- Biblical Foundations for Discernment....................................28
- Cultivating Sensitivity in the Spirit...29
- Fine-Tuning Accuracy through Experience............................29
- Acknowledging and Learning from Mistakes........................30
- Practical Tips for Sharpening Discernment...........................30
- The Ongoing Journey of Discernment....................................30

CHAPTER 4: The Language of Prophecy.....................................32
- Art and Responsibility in Expressing Divine Messages:......32
- The Art of Divine Expression...32
- Scriptural Anchors for Divine Expression.............................33
- Learning from Miscommunication..33
- Guidelines for Expressing Divine Messages..........................33
- Navigating What to Say and What Not to Say......................34
- Decoding Symbols and Metaphors in the Prophetic Journey...........35
- The Language of Symbols...35
- Biblical Anchors for Symbolic Language...............................35
- Examples of Symbolism in Prophetic Communication.......36

- Deciphering Symbols...36
- Personal Encounters with Symbolic Messages.............................37
- Dancing with Divine Metaphors...37
- The Artistry of Prophetic Communication: Mastering the Divine Symphony..38
- Embrace the Divine Flow...38
- Biblical Foundations for Prophetic Communication....................38
- Keys to Mastering Prophetic Communication.............................39
- Crafting Words with Wisdom...39
- Navigating Challenges in Prophetic Communication...................40
- Conclusion: The Symphony Continues..40

CHAPTER 5: Prophetic Intercession and Warfare..............................41
- The Prophetic Intercessor: Bridging Heaven and Earth through Prayer 41
- The Prophet as an Intercessor..42
- Biblical Foundations for Prophetic Intercession..........................42
- Personal Encounters with Prophetic Intercession........................42
- Principles of Prophetic Intercession...43
- Co-laboring with the Divine..44
- The Battlefield of the Prophetic: Engaging in Spiritual Warfare........44
- The Prophetic Battlefield...44
- Biblical Foundations for Spiritual Warfare..................................45
- Attacks on the Prophet..45
- Strategies for Overcoming...46
- Examples of Prophetic Warfare in Scripture................................46
- The Prophetic Weaponry...46
- Victory in the Midst of Battle..47
- Triumph in the Prophetic Battlefield..47

- Unleashing Prophetic Prayer Strategies: A Prophetic Imperative in Ministry..................48
- The Power of Prophetic Prayer..................48
- Biblical Anchors for Prophetic Prayer Strategies..................48
- Prophetic Prayer Strategies in Action..................49
- Personal Insights from Prophetic Prayer Strategies..................49
- Importance of Prophetic Prayer Strategies..................49
- Unveiling Kingdom Realities Through Prophetic Prayer..................50

CHAPTER 6: Navigating Challenges in Prophetic Ministry..................51
- Navigating Challenges: A Prophet's Journey through Pitfalls and Victories..................51
- Personal Encounter: Unveiling the Captive Atmosphere..................51
- Biblical Examples: Prophets Facing Challenges..................52
- Common Pitfalls in Prophetic Ministry..................53
- Overcoming Pitfalls: Strategies for Victory..................53
- The Journey Continues..................54
- Rising from the Ashes: Overcoming Burnout and Discouragement in Prophetic Ministry..................55
- The Shadows of Being Burntout: A Prophetic Reality..................55
- Personal Reflection: When the Flame Flickers Low..................55
- Biblical Anchors: Prophets Navigating Discouragement..................56
- Overcoming Burnout: Strategies for Resilience..................56
- Rising as Eagles from the Abyss..................57
- Embracing Setbacks: A Prophetic Path to Spiritual Growth..................57
- The Prophetic Path: Navigating Setbacks..................58
- Biblical Examples: Prophets Learning from Setbacks..................58
- The Prophetic Pruning: Learning from Missed Marks..................58
- Encouragement to Fellow Prophets: Fear Not the Setbacks..................59
- Setbacks as Stepping Stones..................59

CHAPTER 7: The Prophetic and Leadership..61
- The Tightrope of Authority and Humility: A Prophet's Balancing Act 61
- The Authority of the Prophet: A Divine Mandate:..............................61
- Biblical Anchors: Prophetic Authority and Humility.........................62
- Personal Reflection: Navigating Adoration and Bowing....................62
- Addressing the Bowing Issue: A Lesson from Peter (Acts 10:25-26)..62
- The Problem of Prophetic Elevation..63
- The Prophetic Balancing Act: Strategies for Maintaining Humility...63
- The Sweet Spot of Authority and Humility..63
- The Prophetic Navigator: Guiding the Body of Christ with Divine Direction...64
- The Prophetic Role in the Five-Fold Ministry......................................64
- Distinguishing the Prophet: A Divine Assignment.............................64
- Spiritual Direction: Guiding the Church on God's Path....................65
- Differentiating Prophetic Ministry from Psychic Practices................65
- The Prophet's Caution: Guarding Against Misunderstandings.........66
- Conclusion: Navigating with Divine Precision....................................66

CHAPTER 8: Recognizing False Prophets In A Sea of Voices.................67
- The True Prophet's Mandate: A Divine Charge with Accountability..67
- Distinguishing Traits of False Prophets: A Prophet's Insight.............68
- Personal Encounter: Discerning the Hollow Prophecy......................68
- The Essence of True Prophecy: A Divine Blueprint for Purpose........69
- The Prophet's Call to Discernment: Protecting the Flock..................69
- Guarding the Flock with Discernment..70
- Discerning the Authentic: Navigating the Realm of True Prophecy..70
- Detecting a False Prophet: Warning Signs..70
- Canceling False Prophecies: Empowering the Believer......................71
- The True Prophetic Voice: A Guiding Light...72

CHAPTER 9: The Prophet's Cave: Solitude, Fasting, and Divine Encounter...................73
- Cave: A Prophetic Sojourn into Solitude................73
- Biblical Foundation: Prophetic Encounters in the Wilderness............74
- The Prophet's Isolation: Nurturing Spiritual Intimacy................74
- A Personal Sojourn: Forty Days of Fasting and Divine Presence........74
- Divine Encounter in the Silence: A Prophetic Revelation.................75
- Revelation and Commissioning: The Fruit of Solitude................75
- Emerging from the Cave Renewed................75

CHAPTER 10: Passing the Mantle: The Joy of Equipping Prophetic Voices...................76
- Passing the Mantle: A Legacy of Prophetic Heritage................76
- Biblical Inspiration: The Multiplication of Prophetic Voices............77
- The Joy of Equipping Others: Nurturing Prophetic Gifts.............77
- The Prophet's Joy: Seeing Others Flourish in the Prophetic.............77
- Overcoming Intimidation: Embracing Diversity in the Prophetic.....78
- Multiplying the Symphony of Voices................78
- The Elijah-Elisha Dynamic: A Paradigm for Mentorship................79
- Biblical Foundation: The Transfer of Anointing and Authority (2 Kings 2:9-15)................79
- The Prophetic Call to Mentorship: Nurturing the Next Generation..79
- The Accountability Umbrella: Why Every Prophet Needs a Mentor..80
- Personal Reflection: A Mentor's Impact on My Journey................80
- Overcoming the Fear of Accountability................80
- The Tapestry of Mentorship in the Prophetic................81

CHAPTER 11: The Elijah-Elisha Dynamic: A Paradigm for Mentorship...................82
- Biblical Foundation: The Transfer of Anointing and Authority (2 Kings 2:9-15)................82

- The Prophetic Call to Mentorship: Nurturing the Next Generation..83
- The Accountability Umbrella: Why Every Prophet Needs a Mentor: ..83
- Personal Reflection: A Mentor's Impact on My Journey.....................84
- Overcoming the Fear of Accountability..84
- The Tapestry of Mentorship in the Prophetic......................................84

CHAPTER 12: Stepping into the Prophetic Destiny.............................85
- Reflecting on the Journey...85
- A Prophetic Prayer for Opened Eyes and Ears:...................................86
- A Final Charge..87

ABOUT THE AUTHOR..88

Chapter 1

The Prophetic Call Unveiled

Understanding the Purpose of God's Call to Prophetic Ministry:

In the grand tapestry of God's design, the calling of a prophet emerges as a thread woven with purpose and divine intent. As we embark on this exploration, let us uncover the profound reasons behind why God extends the call to prophetic ministry—a calling that transcends the boundaries of time and resonates across the ages.

Unveiling God's Heart:

At the core of the prophetic calling lies the divine desire to reveal God's heart to His people. Through the prophet's keen sensitivity to the Spirit, the Creator unfolds His character, His plans, and His unyielding love. In every uttered word and revealed vision, the prophet becomes a vessel through which the heartbeat of the Almighty resonates in the ears of humanity.

Guiding and Correcting:

It's important to understand that in the kingdom of God, Prophets are appointed to guide and correct God's people. Throughout history, we witness the prophetic voice steering nations back to righteousness, calling individuals to repentance, and offering divine correction when they veer off the path of God's purpose. The call of a prophet is an anchor that stabilizes the moral compass of societies and individuals alike.

Declaring God's Intentions:

God calls prophets to serve as His spokespersons, articulating His intentions for His people. Whether foretelling future events, proclaiming promises, or revealing warnings, the prophet acts as a divine herald, carrying the weighty responsibility of conveying God's will with clarity and precision.

Bringing Comfort and Hope:

In moments of despair and uncertainty, the prophet serves as a conduit for God's comforting and hopeful messages. Through the prophetic utterances, individuals find solace, reassurance, and a renewed sense of purpose. The call to prophetic ministry, therefore, becomes a channel through which God extends His hand of compassion to uplift the downtrodden.

Calling to Repentance and Transformation:

God calls prophets to herald messages of repentance and transformation. The prophetic voice disrupts complacency, stirring hearts to turn away from sin and embrace righteousness. Through the call, God endeavors to bring about spiritual awakening and renewal within His people.

Establishing Covenant Relationships:

The prophetic calling often involves establishing and reaffirming covenant relationships between God and His people. The prophet becomes a mediator, conveying God's terms and promises, fostering a deeper connection between the Creator and the created.

Anticipating Future Events:

God, in His infinite wisdom, calls prophets to foresee and announce future events. Through these prophetic glimpses, individuals are equipped with insight and preparation for what lies ahead, enabling them to navigate the complexities of life with discernment and faith.

Demonstrating God's Faithfulness:

Ultimately, the call to prophetic ministry serves as a testament to God's faithfulness. By choosing individuals to bear this unique mantle, God demonstrates His unwavering commitment to guide, protect, and shepherd His people through the twists and turns of history.

Dear reader, as you embark on the understanding of God's purpose in calling prophets, may you find inspiration and affirmation in the fact that the divine call is not arbitrary. It is a purposeful, intentional summons aimed at bringing about profound transformation, redemption, and the manifestation of God's glory in the lives of His people.

In the quiet moments of reflection, as I look back on the inception of my journey into the prophetic ministry, I am drawn to the profound realization that the divine call is not merely an event but a sacred encounter—an encounter that has shaped the very fabric of my existence.

The Whisper in the Silence:

The call to prophetic ministry seldom arrives with grandiosity or fanfare. Instead, it often begins as a whisper in the stillness of prayer or a gentle nudge in the depths of the soul. For me, it was an inexplicable yearning—an insatiable hunger to draw closer to the Lord Jesus and to be a vessel for messages beyond my understanding. It was a call that echoed in the silence, urging me to listen with a heart attuned to the frequencies of the spiritual realm.

Navigating the Stirrings:

Understanding the divine call involves a profound exploration of the internal stirrings that precede the outward expression of the prophetic gift. It's a process of self-discovery, a journey into the depths of one's own soul to discern the nuances of the call. There were moments of uncertainty, moments when I questioned whether the whispers were mere figments of my imagination. It was in those moments of doubt that faith became the compass guiding me through the labyrinth of the prophetic call.

The Uniqueness of Each Call:

It's crucial for aspiring prophets to recognize the uniqueness of their call. Just as no two fingerprints are alike, no two prophetic calls are identical. This is why it's important not to compare yourself to any other Prophet or focus too much on the way God uses someone in the Prophetic. The divine tailor crafts each call to fit the individual—customized to one's personality, experiences, and purpose within the Body of Christ. Embracing the individuality of the call fosters authenticity and prevents the trap of comparison.

Embracing the Weight of the Call:

The call to prophetic ministry is weighty. It carries a responsibility that can feel burdensome at times. I vividly recall grappling with the gravity of the call—the realization that I was being entrusted with messages that could shape destinies and transform lives. It's important for emerging prophets to acknowledge the weight, for it is in that acknowledgment that they find strength, humility, and a profound sense of dependence on the One who calls.

Transparency in the Journey:

In my transparency, I confess the moments of reluctance, the times when the call felt inconvenient or overwhelming. It's part of the journey to grapple with the call's demands, and admitting this struggle is not a sign of weakness but an acknowledgment of the refining process inherent in the prophetic journey.

Dear fellow prophets, in understanding the divine call, embrace the uniqueness, navigate the stirrings with faith, and recognize the weightiness of the responsibility. Let the call be your compass, and may your transparency illuminate the path for others walking alongside you. The call is not a destination but a continuous journey, it's a journey of profound encounters, transformation, and a lifelong commitment to being a faithful steward of the prophetic gift.

In the sacred pages of the Scriptures, we find an array of narratives illustrating the profound ways in which God calls individuals into prophetic ministry. These stories are not mere anecdotes but a testament to the divine orchestration that unfolds when the Almighty chooses to speak through chosen vessels. As I delve into these biblical examples, I can't help but reflect on my own calling—a calling that began with a vision of a burning eagle and the resonant voice of the LORD echoing, "I, Jesus, am with you wherever you go." I will explain this vision in further detail later.

Abraham: The Call to a New Land (Genesis 12:1-3):

The divine calling often involves a radical departure from the familiar. In the case of Abraham, the Father of Faith, God called him to leave his homeland and journey to an unknown destination. Similarly, God's call to prophetic ministry may lead us away from the comfortable confines of our current understanding, inviting us to explore uncharted territories of spiritual revelation.

Moses: The Burning Bush Encounter (Exodus 3:1-10):

Moses' call to prophetic leadership came through a burning bush—an awe-inspiring manifestation of God's presence. Just as the bush blazed but was not consumed, the prophetic call is marked by a divine fire that ignites without destroying. It was in the flickering flames of my own vision—the burning eagle—that I sensed the weight of divine presence, an encounter that echoed Moses' commission to lead God's people.

Isaiah: The Vision in the Temple (Isaiah 6:1-8):

Isaiah's commissioning was ushered in by a heavenly vision in the temple, where he witnessed the Lord seated on His throne. The seraphim cried out, "Holy, holy, holy," and Isaiah, overwhelmed by the divine presence, responded, "Here am I. Send me!" The call to prophetic ministry often involves a profound encounter with God's holiness—an encounter that transforms and propels the prophet into a readiness to be sent.

My Vision: The Burning Eagle and the Voice of Jesus:

In the midst of my own journey, I received a vision that etched itself into the tapestry of my prophetic calling. In 2011, several months after giving my life to Christ, one day as I was working out at my local gym in my community, I finished my workout and proceeded out of the building and then I looked up at the sky while walking to my car my spiritual eyes became open. I saw a majestic eagle, engulfed in flames, soaring across the heavens. The intensity of the fire did not consume but radiated strength and resilience. As I beheld this celestial display, the voice of Jesus resounded, affirming His omnipresence: "I, Jesus, am with you wherever you go."

The burning eagle symbolized the refining fire of the Spirit, an emblem of the prophetic journey marked by purification and power. The words of Jesus served as an unshakeable foundation, assuring me that His presence would accompany me through every soaring height and challenging valley of the prophetic ministry.

Understanding the Divine Call:

The divine call to prophetic ministry is not a one-size-fits-all formula. It is a unique encounter, tailored to the individual, and often involves extraordinary manifestations that transcend the natural realm. Whether through visions, dreams, or an audible voice, God's call is unmistakable, leaving an indelible mark on the prophet's soul.

To those discerning the call, immerse yourself in the biblical narratives, understanding that your journey is part of a timeless tapestry woven by the Divine. Just as Abraham, Moses, and Isaiah responded to their calls with faith and obedience, may you too answer the divine summons with a resounding "Here am I. Send me!" Trust that the burning eagle of God's presence will guide you through the soaring heights and the transformative fires of prophetic ministry.

The path of a prophet, though divinely ordained, is not without its trials. The calling to be a spokesperson for the Almighty often attracts opposition and persecution. Yet, it is in these moments of adversity that the true strength of a prophet is revealed.

Understanding the Source of Opposition:

The attacks and persecution faced by prophets are not mere coincidences; they are often rooted in spiritual warfare. The adversary seeks to silence the prophetic voice, knowing its potential to unveil truth and dismantle darkness. Recognizing that the source of opposition is not merely human but spiritual arms, the prophet is equipped with a deeper understanding of the battle at hand.

Scriptural Anchors for Resilience:

- **Corinthians 4:8-9 (NIV):** "We are hard pressed on every side, but not crushed; perplexed, but not in despair; persecuted, but not abandoned; struck down, but not destroyed." This passage encapsulates the essence of a prophet's journey—facing hardships yet remaining unbroken. Knowing that, like Paul, you are not alone in the struggles provides solace and strengthens resolve.
- **Matthew 5:11-12 (ESV):**"Blessed are you when others revile you and persecute you and utter all kinds of evil against you falsely on my account. Rejoice and be glad, for your reward is great in heaven, for so they persecuted the prophets who were before you." Jesus Himself acknowledged the persecution prophets would face. Remembering that this persecution is a sign of alignment with the prophetic legacy helps maintain a perspective focused on eternal rewards.

Strategies for Overcoming Attacks:
- **Firm Identity in Christ:**
- Establish a rock-solid identity rooted in Christ. When attacks come, knowing who you are in Him serves as an unshakeable foundation.

- **Prayer and Spiritual Warfare:**
- Engage in fervent prayer and spiritual warfare. The battles faced are not merely against flesh and blood, and therefore, the weapons employed must be spiritual.
- **Community and Accountability:**
- Surround yourself with a supportive community of believers. Having fellow prophets and allies who understand the unique challenges of the calling provides strength and encouragement.
- **Maintaining Humility:**
- Cultivate humility. In the face of persecution, choosing humility over retaliation disarms the enemy and reflects the character of Christ.
- **Focus on God's Approval:**
- Shift the focus from seeking human approval to seeking God's approval. The validation that comes from knowing you are obedient to His call far surpasses the fleeting affirmation of others.

Perseverance as a Virtue:

The journey of a prophet is not a sprint but a marathon. Perseverance is not only a virtue but a necessity. Holding onto the promises of God, embracing the refining process of persecution, and remaining steadfast in the face of attacks position the prophet to emerge victorious, just as the prophets of old did.

Dear fellow prophets, though the road may be challenging, remember that the One who called you is faithful. Let the scriptural anchors and practical strategies guide you through the storms, and may you emerge stronger, wiser, and even more deeply rooted in the call that sustains you.

As we draw the veil over the exploration of understanding the call of a prophet, we find ourselves standing at the threshold of a profound journey—one that transcends time, culture, and individual lives. The call to prophetic ministry is not a mere selection; it is a divine summoning, an invitation to partner with the Creator in unveiling His purposes on Earth. In reflecting on the multifaceted aspects of this sacred call, we grasp that the divine mandate is woven with threads of revelation, correction, guidance, and comfort. A prophet's role, intricately designed by the hands of the Almighty, extends beyond personal aspirations, reaching into the very fabric of humanity's spiritual tapestry.

Understanding the call is not a stagnant endpoint but a dynamic revelation. It is an ongoing journey of discovery, where each step reveals deeper layers of God's intentions and the intricacies of His divine plan. Just as prophets of old navigated the nuances of their callings, so too do contemporary prophets embark on a path laden with purpose, responsibility, and unparalleled intimacy with the Divine.

May this chapter serve as a compass, guiding you through the realms of revelation and preparing you for the sacred calling that echoes through the corridors of your soul. Whether you are discerning the stirrings of the prophetic within or have long held the mantle of a prophet, know that your journey is interwoven with the very heartbeat of God.

In answering the divine call, embrace the refining fires and the gentle whispers, for they are the nuances of a calling designed with meticulous care. As you tread this path, may you find solace in the assurance that the One who calls is faithful. With every revelation, correction, and comforting word, may your heart resound with the proclamation, "Here am I, Lord. Send me."

Dear prophet, the call is not merely an assignment; it is an invitation to dance in the rhythm of the Divine. May you step into the melody with boldness, grace, and a profound awareness that, in answering the call, you become a vessel through which the Creator orchestrates His symphony of love, redemption, and eternal purpose.

Chapter 2

The Bedrock of Revelation: Building a Solid Spiritual Foundation in the Word of God for Ministry

In the vast landscape of prophetic ministry, there stands an unshakable truth: the strength of one's prophetic calling is intricately tied to the solidity of one's spiritual foundation. As a prophet, I stand witness to the profound impact of grounding oneself in the Word of God—a foundation that withstands the winds of doubt, the storms of uncertainty, and the seismic shifts of life's challenges.

The Word as a Source of Revelation:

The Bible is not merely a book; it is the living, breathing revelation of God's heart. For a prophet, every verse is a portal to divine insights, a wellspring of wisdom waiting to be uncovered. As I have delved into the sacred pages,

I have found that the Word serves as a blueprint for understanding God's character, His plans, and the intricacies of His relationship with His people.

Building Discernment through Scripture:

Discernment, an essential tool in the prophetic arsenal, is honed through the constant intake of God's Word. The more we immerse ourselves in Scripture, the sharper our ability becomes to distinguish between the divine and the deceptive. The Word acts as a filter, sieving through the noise of the world and clarifying the whispers of the Spirit.

Scripture as a Mirror:

In the reflective pool of Scripture, we see not only God's nature but also the reflection of our own hearts. The Word exposes our vulnerabilities, challenges our misconceptions, and molds our character. As a prophet, the journey of self-discovery within the context of God's Word is a crucial aspect of spiritual maturation.

Prayerful Meditation on Scripture:

The act of meditating on Scripture is a sacred practice that transcends mere intellectual understanding. It is an intimate communion with the Divine, a space where the written Word transforms into a personal revelation. As I have spent hours in prayerful meditation, the verses have unfolded like petals, revealing layers of meaning, relevance, and application to my prophetic ministry.

Navigating the Prophetic Path with Scripture:

The prophetic journey is marked by highs and lows, victories and challenges. It is the Word of God that becomes a lamp to our feet and a light to our path (Psalm 119:105). In moments of confusion, I have found clarity in the promises of Scripture. In times of despair, I have discovered hope in the Psalms. The Word, like a compass, directs my steps and anchors my prophetic calling.

Equipping Others with the Word:

As a prophet, part of my calling is to equip others for the journey. In mentoring emerging prophets, I emphasize the indispensable role of the Word in their lives. I encourage them to saturate their minds with Scripture, allowing it to become the lens through which they view the world and the source from which their prophetic utterances flow.

A Prophetic Legacy Built on the Word:

Building a solid spiritual foundation in the Word of God is not a mere recommendation; it is a necessity. The Word is not a passive tool but an active force that shapes, refines, and empowers the prophet for the task at hand. As we stand on the bedrock of Scripture, our prophetic ministry becomes an outpouring of the deep wellsprings of divine revelation, fortified by the timeless truths contained in God's Word. One of my deepest prayers is that every prophet embraces the Word as both guide and sustenance on this sacred journey.

Crafting and Upholding a Godly Identity in Prophetic Ministry:

As a prophet navigating the ethereal realms of divine revelation, I am acutely aware that the strength of my ministry is inseparable from the fabric of my character. The importance of building and maintaining a Godly character in the prophetic journey is not a mere suggestion; it is an imperative etched into the very essence of the calling.

The Crucible of Character:

Character, the sum of our moral and ethical qualities, is the crucible where the authenticity of our prophetic ministry is tested. A solid character, rooted in godliness, serves as a beacon in the dark, guiding not only ourselves but those who look to us for spiritual guidance.

Personal Temptations and Triumphs:

In the shadow of the prophetic mantle, I have encountered the formidable adversary of temptation. The allure of pride, the seduction of acclaim, and the whisper of compromise have sought to undermine the integrity of my character. There were moments when the weight of the prophetic call seemed to justify shortcuts, yet it was in those very moments that the refining fires of character development burned the brightest. Every prophet will encounter moments in ministry that temps them to compromise, but holding on to their integrity in the Lord through their personal relationships will give them strength to counter these temptations.

Scriptural Wisdom on Character:

- **Proverbs 4:23 (NIV):** "Above all else, guard your heart, for everything you do flows from it." This proverb encapsulates the core of character—our actions, words, and prophecies emanate from the wellspring of our hearts. Guarding our hearts ensures the purity of our character.
- **Galatians 5:22-23 (ESV):** "But the fruit of the Spirit is love, joy, peace, patience, kindness, goodness, faithfulness, gentleness, self-control; against such things there is no law." The fruits of the Spirit are not just poetic ideals; they are the tangible markers of a godly character. Every prophet should aspire to bear this fruit abundantly.
- **1 Timothy 3:1-7 (NIV):** "Here is a trustworthy saying: Whoever aspires to be an overseer desires a noble task. Now the overseer is to be above reproach, faithful to his wife, temperate, self-controlled, respectable, hospitable, able to teach..." Though written specifically for overseers, these qualities are universally applicable to anyone in leadership, including those in prophetic ministry.

Balancing Visibility and Humility:

The prophetic mantle often carries with it a level of visibility. While visibility is not inherently negative, it becomes precarious when it fosters pride or a sense of entitlement. Maintaining a humble heart, acknowledging that every prophetic gift is a divine deposit, safeguards the character from the corrosive effects of pride.

A Legacy of Godly Character:

The importance of building and maintaining a Godly character in prophetic ministry is not just a personal discipline—it is a legacy we leave for generations to come. A prophetic voice resonates most powerfully when it emerges from a character shaped by the hands of the Divine. May every prophet understand that, as we craft a Godly character, we contribute to a rich tapestry that reflects the beauty of the One who called us into this sacred journey.

Prioritizing the Fruit of the Spirit over the Gifts in Prophetic Ministry:

In the pulsating heart of prophetic ministry, a profound truth emerges — the enduring legacy of a prophetic calling rests not solely on the grandeur of spiritual gifts but on the richness of the fruit of the Spirit. I myself have treaded both the realms of gifting and character, and have found out that it's very significant to a prophet in their ministry to prioritize the fruit over the gifts. I truly believe that is the secret to a successful and enduring prophetic ministry. I often say that the Bible says your gift will make room for you and bring you before great men, but your character, which is the fruit of the Spirit is what is going to keep you with those great men.

The Distinction Between Gifts and Fruit:

In the landscape of the Spirit, gifts are bestowed, and fruit is cultivated. The gifts are the manifestations of the Spirit's power, while the fruit is the evidence of the Spirit's work within. Both are indispensable, yet the fruit, borne out of the character, is the tapestry that weaves together the longevity and impact of a prophet's ministry.

Scriptural Foundations:

- **1 Corinthians 13:1-3 (NIV):** "If I speak in the tongues of men or of angels, but do not have love, I am only a resounding gong or a clanging cymbal. If I have the gift of prophecy and can fathom all mysteries and all knowledge, and if I have a faith that can move mountains, but do not have love, I am nothing." These verses from Corinthians unequivocally emphasize that without love — a fruit of the Spirit — even the loftiest spiritual gifts lose their significance.
- **Galatians 5:22-23 (ESV):** "But the fruit of the Spirit is love, joy, peace, patience, kindness, goodness, faithfulness, gentleness, self-control; against such things, there is no law." The list of the fruit of the Spirit is an inventory of qualities that form the bedrock of a godly character, each contributing to the success and longevity of a prophetic ministry.

The Transient Nature of Gifts:

Gifts, while awe-inspiring and impactful, can sometimes be fleeting. The spectacular manifestations that accompany the gifts can inadvertently become the focus, leading to a performance-driven ministry. Yet, like a passing comet, the brilliance diminishes, leaving behind the question of lasting impact.

Fruit as the Sustaining Force:

The fruit of the Spirit, on the other hand, is the sustaining force in the life of a prophet. Love, joy, peace, and the other attributes are not contingent on circumstances or momentary manifestations. They are the steady undercurrent that fuels the longevity of a ministry, creating a foundation that stands firm even in the face of storms.

Character as a Magnet for the Anointing:

A godly character, adorned with the fruit of the Spirit, becomes a magnetic force for the anointing. The Spirit delights to dwell in vessels marked by love, kindness, and humility. A character steeped in the fruit of the Spirit attracts the presence of God, and where His presence abides, the fullness of His power and gifts are made manifest.

Building a Lasting Legacy:

In prioritizing the fruit of the Spirit over the gifts, a prophet establishes the cornerstone of a lasting legacy. The impact of a ministry is not measured by momentary spectacular displays but by the transformed lives, the seeds of love and kindness planted, and the enduring influence on generations to come.

A Symphony of Fruit and Gifts:

In the grand symphony of prophetic ministry, let the gifts resonate, but may the fruit be the harmonious melody that captivates hearts and echoes through eternity. For it is in the cultivation of godly character, adorned with the fruit of the Spirit, that a prophet ensures not just a successful ministry but a legacy that reverberates through the corridors of time. May every prophet heed the call to prioritize the fruit over the gifts, understanding that it is in the soil of godly character that the most enduring and fruitful prophetic trees take root.

CHAPTER 3

Recognizing the Voice of God

In the vast symphony of existence, discerning the distinct cadence of the Divine voice is both an art and a sacred journey. I will truly say from the from my years of experience in walking the Lord Jesus the ability to recognize God's voice is not just a skill; it is the cornerstone of the prophetic calling. In this chapter, I invite you to explore the nuances of recognizing the voice of God — a melody that resonates through the corridors of the spirit.

Creating Space for Divine Dialogue:

Recognizing the voice of God begins with cultivating an environment for communion. In the stillness of prayer, the tumult of the world fades, and the divine conversation begins. Establish a sacred space where your heart is attuned to His frequency, and where you can listen without distraction.

Biblical Anchors for Recognition:

- **John 10:27 (NIV):** "My sheep listen to my voice; I know them, and they follow me." Acknowledge your identity as one of His sheep. Embrace the intimacy of being known by the Shepherd and the reciprocal act of listening and following.
- **Isaiah 30:21 (NIV):** "Whether you turn to the right or to the left, your ears will hear a voice behind you, saying, 'This is the way; walk in it.'" God's guidance is not arbitrary; it is intentional. Train your spiritual ears to discern the voice that directs and illuminates the path.

Distinguishing God's Voice from Others:

In the vast chorus of spiritual voices, recognizing the timbre of the Divine requires discernment. God's voice is characterized by truth, love, and alignment with His Word. Practice distinguishing His voice from the cacophony of competing narratives, ensuring that the resonance is harmonious with His character.

The Language of Love:

God's voice is the language of love. It may manifest as a gentle whisper, a comforting impression, or an unexpected prompting. Embrace the diversity of His communication, understanding that the Creator employs myriad expressions to convey His messages.

Testing the Alignment with Scripture:

The Word of God serves as the benchmark for recognizing His voice. Any message or impression must align with the principles and truths contained in Scripture. A prophet grounded in the Word is equipped to discern the authentic voice of the Shepherd.

Personal Experiences and Lessons:

I vividly recall a moment when I received what I believed to be a profound revelation. The excitement of the encounter clouded my discernment, and I hastily shared the message without seeking confirmation. It became evident later that my eagerness had outpaced divine timing, and the message was premature.

From this experience, I learned the importance of patience and the necessity of seeking confirmation before declaring a prophetic word. It underscored the truth that recognizing God's voice involves a delicate balance of attentiveness and restraint, a lesson etched into the fabric of my prophetic journey.

Practical Steps for Recognition:
- **Consistent Prayer and Meditation:**
- Establish a regular rhythm of prayer and meditation, creating a space for divine conversation.
- **Familiarity with Scripture:**
- Immerse yourself in the Word of God. The more acquainted you are with His written voice, the more attuned you become to His spoken voice.

- **Seeking Confirmation:**
- Before declaring a prophetic message, seek confirmation through prayer and, if possible, consult with trusted mentors or peers.

The Symphony of Divine Communication:

Recognizing the voice of God is a journey of intimacy, discernment, and alignment with His Word. As a prophet, your ability to distinguish His voice amidst the spiritual symphony is not just a gift; it's a responsibility. May you embark on this sacred journey with humility, eager ears, and a heart attuned to the gentle whispers that guide you into the depth of divine dialogue.

Cultivating a Lifestyle of Sensitivity:

To hear God's voice requires a lifestyle steeped in sensitivity to the Spirit. It's about creating sacred spaces for communion, moments where the hustle and bustle of the world fade into the background, and the still, small voice of God becomes the focal point. Regular prayer, meditation, and intentional seeking are the foundational building blocks of a prophetic lifestyle.

Biblical Insights into Hearing God:

- **1 Kings 19:12 (NIV):** "After the earthquake came a fire, but the Lord was not in the fire. And after the fire came a gentle whisper." Learn from Elijah's encounter. God's voice may not always be in the grand and spectacular but often in the gentle and subtle. Train your spirit to discern the soft whispers amid life's clamor.

Embracing Visions and Dreams:

Visions and dreams are portals through which God unveils His mysteries. Create an atmosphere conducive to receiving these revelations. Journal your dreams, pay attention to recurring themes, and seek God's interpretation. Be open to the symbolism He uses to convey messages, knowing that God often speaks in a language beyond our comprehension.

Hearing the Audible Voice:

While hearing the audible voice of God may not be an everyday occurrence, it is an extraordinary experience that demands attentive listening. To attune yourself, practice active listening in prayer. Be patient, allow moments of stillness, and be prepared for the unexpected. God may choose to speak audibly when the atmosphere is conducive for such encounters.

Learning from Mistakes:

Even in the journey of a prophet, mistakes can become profound teachers. I recall a time when I misinterpreted a vision, proclaiming a message with unwarranted certainty. The repercussions were humbling, but in the aftermath, I discovered the beauty of humility and the importance of double-checking the interpretations I receive.

In this instance, I learned the significance of seeking confirmation and being cautious about hastily delivering a message without thorough discernment. It taught me the invaluable lesson of humility and the weightiness of the prophetic responsibility. Every mistake, when approached with a humble heart, becomes a stepping stone to greater accuracy and understanding.

Tips for Growth:
- **Frequent the Scriptures:**
- Immerse yourself in the Word of God. The more acquainted you are with His written word, the easier it becomes to recognize His voice.
- **Practice Discernment:**
- Train yourself to discern the nuances of God's voice. Distinguish His voice from the myriad of competing voices in the spiritual realm.
- **Seek Accountability:**
- Surround yourself with trusted mentors and peers who can provide guidance, correction, and confirmation in your prophetic journey.
- **Remain Teachable:**
- Cultivate a teachable spirit. Recognize that growth in the prophetic is a continuous journey, and every experience, whether success or failure, contributes to your development.

The Symphony of God's Voice:

As you embark on the journey of sharpening your prophetic ear, remember that hearing God's voice is an ongoing relationship rather than a destination. It is a symphony, a harmonious collaboration between the divine and the human spirit. May you walk in the confidence that, as you seek to hear God with increasing clarity, the melodies of His voice will become the guiding soundtrack of your prophetic journey.

The Art of Discernment: Sharpening Your Prophetic Sensitivity for Accuracy

In the intricate dance of the prophetic, discernment is the compass that guides the prophet through the diverse landscapes of the spiritual realm. From the vantage point of a seasoned prophet, this chapter unfolds the layers of the discernment journey — a pilgrimage towards heightened sensitivity in the spirit, where accuracy becomes not just a goal but a way of life.

Understanding the Essence of Discernment:

Discernment is the keystone of prophetic accuracy. It is the ability to perceive and understand the subtle nuances of the spirit realm. Just as a skilled musician distinguishes between various notes in a symphony, a prophet with sharpened discernment navigates through the frequencies of the spiritual realm with precision.

Biblical Foundations for Discernment:

- **Hebrews 5:14 (NIV):** "But solid food is for the mature, who by constant use have trained themselves to distinguish good from evil." Discernment is a discipline honed through constant practice. It is the mark of spiritual maturity, requiring diligence and commitment.
- **1 Corinthians 12:10 (NIV):** "to another the working of miracles, to another prophecy, to another the ability to distinguish between spirits, to another various kinds of tongues, to another the interpretation of tongues." Discernment is listed among the spiritual gifts, emphasizing its vital role in the prophetic ministry.

Cultivating Sensitivity in the Spirit:
- **Fasting and Prayer:**
- Engage in periods of fasting and intensified prayer. Fasting clears the spiritual clutter, making room for heightened sensitivity. It is a discipline that fortifies your spirit and attunes it to the frequencies of the Divine.
- **Immerse Yourself in the Word:**
- The Word of God is a discerning tool. Regularly immerse yourself in Scripture. The more acquainted you are with God's written word, the more attuned you become to His voice and the discernment of spirits.
- **Maintain a Posture of Humility:**
- Discernment thrives in the soil of humility. Acknowledge your reliance on the Holy Spirit for insight, and be open to correction. A humble heart is receptive to the gentle whispers of discernment.
- **Surround Yourself with Discerning Community:**
- Forge connections with like-minded individuals who prioritize discernment. A community that shares insights, challenges, and confirms discernments contributes to collective growth.

Fine-Tuning Accuracy through Experience:

Accuracy in discernment is a journey, not an instant achievement. With each encounter and experience, your spiritual senses become more finely tuned. Be deliberate in reflecting on past discernments — both accurate and inaccurate — and use them as building blocks for growth.

Acknowledging and Learning from Mistakes:

Every prophet, no matter how seasoned, encounters moments of misinterpretation. I recall an instance where my discernment led me astray, and I spoke prematurely on a matter. It served as a humbling reminder that even the most attuned prophets are susceptible to missteps. In retrospect, I recognized the importance of patient waiting and seeking confirmation.

Practical Tips for Sharpening Discernment:

- **Regular Self-Examination:**
- Set aside time for self-reflection. Regularly assess the state of your heart, motives, and potential biases that may influence your discernment.
- **Journaling Experiences:**
- Keep a prophetic journal. Document your encounters, dreams, and discernments. Over time, patterns and themes may emerge, providing insights into the nuances of your discernment.
- **Seek Confirmation:**
- Before delivering a prophetic word, seek confirmation through prayer and, if possible, consultation with trusted prophetic mentors or peers.

The Ongoing Journey of Discernment:

In conclusion, the art of discernment is not a destination but a journey. It's a continuous refining process where sensitivity in the spirit deepens with each step. As you commit to cultivating discernment, may your journey be marked by humility, a hunger for God's Word, and a willingness to learn from both successes and mistakes. In the pursuit of accuracy, let discernment become not just a skill but a lifestyle that enriches your prophetic journey and draws you ever closer to the heart of the Lord Jesus Christ.

CHAPTER 4

The Language Of Prophecy

Art and Responsibility in Expressing Divine Messages:

In the realm of prophecy, conveying divine messages is both an art and a responsibility that carries profound weight. As a prophet, the manner in which these messages are articulated is paramount. This chapter delves into the nuances of expressing divine messages correctly, drawing insights from both successful and challenging moments in the prophetic journey.

The Art of Divine Expression:

Conveying a divine message requires a delicate balance of clarity, humility, and sensitivity. The prophet serves as a vessel, entrusted with the sacred task of accurately representing the heart and intentions of the Divine. The expression is not just in the words spoken but in the spirit with which they are shared.

Scriptural Anchors for Divine Expression:
- **Colossians 4:6 (NIV):** "Let your conversation be always full of grace, seasoned with salt, so that you may know how to answer everyone." The choice of words is an art. Like seasoning, they should enhance and bring out the flavor without overpowering the message.
- **Proverbs 15:1 (NIV):** "A gentle answer turns away wrath, but a harsh word stirs up anger." The tone of communication is as crucial as the message itself. A gentle and respectful demeanor opens hearts to receive the divine word.

Learning from Miscommunication:

I recall a specific instance where I received a profound revelation during prayer. However, in my eagerness to share the message, I failed to convey it with the necessary nuance. The impact was not what I had anticipated; instead of inspiring, it led to confusion and even resistance.

This experience taught me a vital lesson: the importance of pausing, seeking the guidance of the Holy Spirit, and carefully choosing the words that encapsulate the divine message. It underscored the truth that even a genuine word from God can lose its potency if not expressed with wisdom and discernment.

Guidelines for Expressing Divine Messages:
- **Prayerful Preparation:**
- Before expressing a divine message, spend time in prayer. Seek clarity, discern the spirit behind the message, and ask for guidance on how to articulate it effectively.
- **Discernment of Timing:**

- Timing is crucial in the prophetic. Not every message needs to be delivered immediately. Discern the appropriate season, and trust in divine timing.
- **Cautious Language:**
- Be cautious with language. Choose words that convey the message without causing unnecessary confusion or offense. Strive for simplicity, avoiding jargon that may alienate or confuse the audience.
- **Check Your Motives:**
- Examine your motives before expressing a divine message. Ensure that pride, personal agenda, or a desire for attention are not clouding the purity of the message.

Navigating What to Say and What Not to Say:
- **Listen to the Holy Spirit:**
- Cultivate a sensitive ear to the promptings of the Holy Spirit. He will guide you on what to say and what to withhold, ensuring that the message aligns with the divine intention.
- **Filter Through Love:**
- Love should be the filtering lens for every prophetic word. If the message lacks love or humility, it may not be the right time or the right words.
- **Seek Confirmation:**
- Before sharing a significant message, seek confirmation through prayer and, if possible, consultation with trusted mentors or peers. Confirmation adds a layer of assurance.

Expressing divine messages is a sacred dance that requires both skill and reverence. As a prophet, you are not just a mouthpiece; you are an artist painting the canvas of hearts with the brushstrokes of God's intentions. May your words carry the weight of the divine, expressed with grace, humility, and an unwavering commitment to the sacred responsibility of prophetic expression.

Decoding Symbols and Metaphors in the Prophetic Journey:

In the realm of prophecy, the language of symbols and metaphors is the divine tapestry through which God paints profound truths. As a prophet, the ability to decipher these symbolic messages is not merely a skill; it is an essential facet of navigating the intricate landscapes of the prophetic journey.

The Language of Symbols:

Symbols are the currency of divine communication, a language that transcends the limitations of mere words. God often uses symbols to convey multifaceted messages, each layer unfolding a new dimension of revelation. Just as a skilled artist imbues their work with symbolism, so too does the Lord infuse His messages with rich and nuanced meaning.

Biblical Anchors for Symbolic Language:
- **Genesis 40:8 (NIV):** "We both had dreams," they answered, "but there is no one to interpret them." Then Joseph said to them, "Do not interpretations belong to God? Tell me your dreams." Joseph, the patriarch with a prophetic gifting, recognized that interpretations belong to God. He understood the language of dreams, which often involves symbolic elements.
- **Ezekiel 12:6 (NIV):** "During the day, while they are watching, bring out your belongings packed for exile. Then in the evening, while they are watching, go out like those who go into exile." God frequently

instructed prophets, like Ezekiel, to convey messages through symbolic actions, each carrying a profound meaning.

Examples of Symbolism in Prophetic Communication:

- **Animals:**
- Animals are recurring symbols in prophetic visions. For instance, a lion may represent strength and authority (Revelation 5:5), a lamb portrays innocence and sacrifice (John 1:29), and an eagle symbolizes vision, swiftness, and transcendence (Isaiah 40:31).
- **Colors:**
- Colors often carry symbolic significance. White symbolizes purity and holiness, red signifies sacrifice and blood, and blue represents the heavenly or divine. These are just a few to give you as you continue to pray and grow in grace the Holy Spirit will reveal and teach you more.
- **Numbers:**
- Numbers hold symbolic meaning in the prophetic realm. Seven, for example, represents completeness and perfection (Genesis 2:2), while twelve symbolizes divine government and the twelve tribes of Israel.
- **Objects and Actions:**
- Even mundane objects and actions can carry profound symbolic weight. A broken jar may signify judgment or the shattering of a covenant (Jeremiah 19:10), and walking barefoot might represent humility or a significant message (Isaiah 20:2-4).

Deciphering Symbols:
- **Seek the Holy Spirit's Guidance:**

- The Holy Spirit is the divine interpreter. Before attempting to decipher symbols, seek His guidance through prayer and meditation. Invite Him to unveil the layers of meaning embedded in the symbols.
- **Scriptural Reference:**
- Consult the Bible for references to similar symbols. Scripture often provides clues and patterns that aid in understanding the symbolic language used by God.
- **Context Matters:**
- Pay attention to the context of the vision or message. The meaning of a symbol can vary based on the broader narrative in which it appears.

Personal Encounters with Symbolic Messages:

In my own prophetic journey, I once received a vision of a vine laden with various fruits. Through prayer and meditation, I discerned that the vine represented the Church, and each fruit symbolized different aspects of spiritual growth and ministry. The vision served as a call to nurture and cultivate the diverse giftings within the body of believers.

Dancing with Divine Metaphors:

Understanding symbols and metaphors in the prophetic is akin to dancing with divine metaphors. It requires a keen sensitivity, a heart open to the whispers of the Spirit, and a commitment to unraveling the layers of meaning woven into the symbolic tapestry. As a prophet, may you approach these symbols with humility and reverence, knowing that each stroke of divine imagery carries a message crafted by the hands of the Master Artist.

The Artistry of Prophetic Communication: Mastering the Divine Symphony:

In the sacred realm of the prophetic, communication is not just the conveyance of words; it is an art, a dance with the divine rhythm that resonates through the corridors of the spirit. As a prophet, mastering the art of prophetic communication is an ongoing journey of refinement, attunement, and submission to the divine flow.

Embrace the Divine Flow:

Prophetic communication is not a monologue; it's a dialogue with the divine. Embrace the rhythm of the Spirit, allowing His currents to guide your words and expressions. Like a skilled dancer yielding to the music, let your communication be a graceful response to the orchestration of the Holy Spirit.

Biblical Foundations for Prophetic Communication:
- **Jeremiah 1:9 (NIV):** "Then the Lord reached out his hand and touched my mouth and said to me, 'I have put my words in your mouth.'" The divine touch is the essence of prophetic communication. Allow God to touch your lips and infuse His words into your being.
- **1 Corinthians 2:13 (NIV):** "This is what we speak, not in words taught us by human wisdom but in words taught by the Spirit, explaining spiritual realities with Spirit-taught words." Prophetic communication transcends human wisdom. It is a collaboration with the Spirit, articulating spiritual realities with words inspired by the Lord.

Keys to Mastering Prophetic Communication:
- **Cultivate Intimacy with God:**
- The depth of your communication is directly proportional to the depth of your intimacy with God. Spend time in His presence, cultivating a relationship that becomes the wellspring of your prophetic utterances.
- **Sensitivity to the Spirit:**
- Develop a keen sensitivity to the promptings of the Holy Spirit. Prophetic communication is a partnership, and being attuned to His lead ensures that your words align with His intentions.
- **Submit to Divine Timing:**
- Timing is an integral aspect of prophetic communication. Submit to divine timing, recognizing that not every revelation needs immediate expression. Be patient, allowing God to unfold His plans in His perfect time.
- **Practice Active Listening:**
- Prophetic communication involves not just speaking but also listening. Actively listen to the whispers of the Spirit, to the needs and questions of the people, and to the broader context in which you are called to communicate.

Crafting Words with Wisdom:
- **Choose Your Words Deliberately:**
- Every word carries weight in the prophetic. Choose your words deliberately, recognizing their potential impact on hearts and lives.
- **Balance Authority with Humility:**
- While conveying the authority of the divine message, balance it with humility. Recognize that you are a vessel chosen by God, and the authority lies in the message, not in the messenger.
- **Adapt Your Communication Style:**

- Different situations and audiences call for varying communication styles. Be adaptable, allowing the Spirit to guide you in tailoring your message to resonate with the hearts of those who hear.

Navigating Challenges in Prophetic Communication:

In the tapestry of prophetic communication, challenges may arise. There might be instances when the message is met with resistance or misunderstood. In these moments, remain anchored in humility, open to correction, and reliant on the grace that covers imperfections.

Conclusion: The Symphony Continues:

As a prophet, your role in the divine symphony of communication is both an honor and a responsibility. Mastering the art of prophetic communication is a lifelong pursuit, a continuous refinement of the vessel through which the divine melodies are expressed. May your journey be marked by a surrendered heart, a listening ear, and a voice that echoes the harmonies of heaven. In the ongoing symphony of prophetic communication, may you find yourself not just a participant but a cherished instrument in the hands of the Master Composer.

CHAPTER 5

Prophetic Intercession and Warfare

The Prophetic Intercessor: Bridging Heaven and Earth through Prayer

In the intricate dance between the heavens and the earth, the prophet stands as a bridge, a conduit through which divine intervention touches the earthly realm. The role of a prophet in intercession is not merely a task; it's a sacred assignment to partner with God in shaping the destinies of individuals, nations, and the world. In this section, we delve into the profound role of the prophet as an intercessor, I'll be drawing from personal experiences, biblical examples, and the awe-inspiring moments when prayer shifted the course of events in my life and ministry. I pray that this portion of the prayer really intensifies your passion for prayer and intercession. I strongly believe that prayer and intercession are the nucleus of the function of a Prophet.

The Prophet as an Intercessor:

Intercession is the heartbeat of the prophetic ministry. It is the act of standing in the gap, lifting the concerns of humanity before the throne of God, and being a voice that echoes the desires of heaven on earth. As a prophet, intercession is not an option; it's an integral part of the divine calling.

Biblical Foundations for Prophetic Intercession:
- **Ezekiel 22:30 (NIV):** "I looked for someone among them who would build up the wall and stand before me in the gap on behalf of the land so I would not have to destroy it, but I found no one." The imagery of standing in the gap is vivid in this passage. The prophet is called to intercede, to be a bulwark against destruction through prayer.
- **James 5:16 (NIV):** "Therefore confess your sins to each other and pray for each other so that you may be healed. The prayer of a righteous person is powerful and effective." The effectiveness of the prophet's prayer is rooted in righteousness. The intercessory role requires a commitment to righteous living and a heart aligned with God's will.

Personal Encounters with Prophetic Intercession:

In my own journey as a prophet, there have been moments when the burden of intercession pressed upon me with an intensity that could not be ignored. I vividly recall a season of prayer for a community facing economic hardships. As I poured out my heart in intercession, a deep sense of peace settled upon me. In the weeks that followed, doors of opportunity began to open, and the economic situation in that community experienced a notable shift.

These experiences are a testament to the power of prophetic intercession — moments when the Spirit moves in response to prayers offered in alignment with divine purposes.

Principles of Prophetic Intercession:
- **Listening to the Spirit:**
- Prophetic intercession begins with listening. The prophet must attune their ear to the promptings of the Holy Spirit, discerning the specific concerns that God desires to address through prayer.
- **Praying with Authority:**
- The prophet carries a unique authority in intercession. It is not a position of arrogance but a recognition of the divine commission to stand before God on behalf of others. Pray with the authority that comes from knowing your identity and calling.
- **Aligning with God's Heart:**
- Effective intercession flows from a heart aligned with God's heart. It involves sharing His burdens, echoing His desires, and standing in agreement with His plans for redemption and restoration.
- **Biblical Examples of Prophetic Intercession:**
- **Moses (Exodus 32:11-14):**
- Moses stood in the gap for the rebellious Israelites, entreating God not to destroy them. His intercession resulted in God relenting from His initial intention.
- **Elijah (1 Kings 18:41-46):**
- Elijah's intercession for rain after a prolonged drought was marked by persistence and faith. His posture of prayer ushered in the promised rain.

Co-laboring with the Divine:

In the divine tapestry of intercession, the prophet is not a detached observer but a co-laborer with the Divine. Through prayer, the prophet aligns with God's redemptive purposes, participates in the unfolding drama of salvation, and becomes an instrument of transformation.

May the prophet, as an intercessor, embrace the gravity and privilege of this role. In the quiet moments of prayer, may the spirit of intercession fall afresh, ushering in the miraculous, shifting the spiritual atmosphere, and establishing a divine connection between heaven and earth. As the prophet intercedes, may they witness the transformative power of prayer that not only shifts circumstances but opens portals for God's glory to manifest in the midst of His people.

The Battlefield of the Prophetic: Engaging in Spiritual Warfare:

In the realm of the prophetic, the call to serve as a spiritual sentinel often comes hand in hand with the reality of engaging in spiritual warfare. The prophet, with eyes attuned to both the celestial and terrestrial, is a frontline warrior against the forces of darkness.

The Prophetic Battlefield:

The prophetic journey is inherently intertwined with spiritual warfare. As the bearer of divine messages and revelations, the prophet is a threat to the kingdom of darkness. Attacks may manifest in various forms — from personal struggles to opposition from external forces. The spiritual battlefield is a testing ground for the prophet's resilience, faith, and dependence on the God of victory.

Biblical Foundations for Spiritual Warfare:

- **Ephesians 6:12 (NIV):** "For our struggle is not against flesh and blood, but against the rulers, against the authorities, against the powers of this dark world and against the spiritual forces of evil in the heavenly realms." This foundational scripture underscores the spiritual nature of the battle. The prophet is not contending against mere human adversaries but against unseen forces in the heavenly realms.
- **2 Corinthians 10:4-5 (NIV):** "The weapons we fight with are not the weapons of the world. On the contrary, they have divine power to demolish strongholds. We demolish arguments and every pretension that sets itself up against the knowledge of God, and we take captive every thought to make it obedient to Christ." The prophetic arsenal is divinely empowered, capable of demolishing strongholds and confronting the intellectual and spiritual opposition to God's truth.

Attacks on the Prophet:
- **Personal Struggles:**
- Prophets often face intense personal struggles, including doubts, discouragement, and attacks on their identity and calling.
- **Opposition from Religious Spirits:**
- The religious spirit seeks to distort the pure message of the prophet, introducing legalism, tradition, and resistance to change.
- **Interference in Relationships:**
- The enemy may target relationships, seeking to sow discord, misunderstanding, or isolation, hindering the prophet's effectiveness.

Strategies for Overcoming:
- **Cloaked in the Armor of God:**
- Embrace the full armor of God as outlined in Ephesians 6:13-17. Each piece — the belt of truth, breastplate of righteousness, shoes of peace, shield of faith, helmet of salvation, and sword of the Spirit — provides vital protection against the spiritual onslaught.
- **Firm Foundation in God's Word:**
- Ground yourself in the unshakeable truths of God's Word. The Bible serves as a reliable compass in the midst of spiritual warfare, providing guidance and discernment.
- **Prayer and Intercession:**
- Engage in fervent, strategic prayer and intercession. The prophet's prayers are not just defensive but offensive weapons, tearing down demonic strongholds and releasing God's power.

Examples of Prophetic Warfare in Scripture:

- **Elijah on Mount Carmel (1 Kings 18):**
- Elijah's confrontation with the prophets of Baal is a vivid illustration of prophetic warfare. His prayers, coupled with bold actions, led to the defeat of the false prophets and a manifestation of God's power.
- **Daniel's Persistent Prayer (Daniel 10):**
- Daniel's three weeks of fasting and prayer resulted in the defeat of the spiritual opposition (the prince of Persia) and the release of angelic reinforcements.

The Prophetic Weaponry:
- **Decreeing and Declaring:**

- Prophets possess the authority to decree and declare God's will. By speaking forth divine truths, they release power that shapes spiritual and earthly realities.
- **Prophetic Acts:**
- Engaging in prophetic acts, like the symbolic actions of biblical prophets, can shift spiritual atmospheres and challenge the dominion of darkness.
- **Spirit-Led Discernment:**
- The prophet's discernment, sharpened through the Holy Spirit, pierces through deception and reveals the schemes of the enemy.

Victory in the Midst of Battle:

Victory in spiritual warfare is not a distant hope but a present reality for the prophetic warrior. The battles fought and won on the spiritual frontlines pave the way for the manifestation of God's glory in the natural realm.

Triumph in the Prophetic Battlefield:

The prophet, armed with divine authority and equipped with spiritual weaponry, stands as a formidable force in the battlefield of spiritual warfare. Through prayer, discernment, and strategic engagement, the prophetic voice becomes a catalyst for dismantling satanic strongholds and advancing the kingdom of God.

May the prophet embrace their role as a warrior, knowing that the battle is not theirs alone but the Lord's. In the midst of spiritual warfare, may they emerge not only victorious but transformed — refined, strengthened, and ever more attuned to the heartbeat of the Lord Jesus Christ.

Unleashing Prophetic Prayer Strategies: A Prophetic Imperative in Ministry

In the tapestry of prophetic ministry, prayer is not just a ritual; it is a strategic weapon, a dynamic force that shapes destinies and dismantles strongholds. As a prophet, the utilization of prophetic prayer strategies is not merely a recommendation; it is an imperative, a divine mandate to partner with God in transforming lives and nations.

The Power of Prophetic Prayer:

Prophetic prayer is not a monologue; it is a dialogue with the Lord. It is a partnership with the Holy Spirit, aligning our prayers with God's purposes and releasing His will into the earth. Prophetic prayer strategies involve intentional, Spirit-led approaches to intercession that go beyond routine supplications.

Biblical Anchors for Prophetic Prayer Strategies:
- **2 Chronicles 7:14 (NIV):** "If my people, who are called by my name, will humble themselves and pray and seek my face and turn from their wicked ways, then I will hear from heaven, and I will forgive their sin and will heal their land." This foundational scripture reveals the transformative power of strategic, repentant prayer. It is a blueprint for prophetic intercession that impacts both individuals and nations.
- **Daniel's Strategic Prayer (Daniel 9:3-19):**
- Daniel's prayer in chapter 9 is a masterclass in prophetic intercession. He strategically aligns his prayers with the Word of God, confessing sin, and seeking divine mercy for the restoration of Jerusalem.

Prophetic Prayer Strategies in Action:

- **Identifying Strongholds:**
- Prophetic prayer involves discerning spiritual strongholds that hinder the advancement of God's Kingdom. Through prayer, seek revelation about specific areas in need of a breakthrough, whether in personal lives, communities, or nations.
- **Praying in Alignment with God's Word:**
- Craft prayers that align with the promises and principles found in God's Word. Prophetic prayer strategies are rooted in the Scriptures, wielding the Word as a sword against the schemes of the enemy.
- **Strategic Declarations and Decrees:**
- Prophets have the authority to declare and decree God's will. Strategically frame prayers as declarations, releasing the power of God's spoken Word to shape circumstances and bring about transformation.

Personal Insights from Prophetic Prayer Strategies:

In my own journey, I've witnessed the transformative impact of strategic prayers. There was a season of intense spiritual warfare over a community gripped by addiction and despair. Through discernment and strategic prophetic prayer, specific strongholds were identified, and targeted intercession led to visible breakthroughs. Lives were transformed, chains were broken, and a tangible shift occurred in the spiritual atmosphere.

Importance of Prophetic Prayer Strategies:
- **Strategic Focus:**

- Prophetic prayer strategies provide focus in intercession. Instead of generic petitions, they target specific needs, aligning with God's purposes for a more effective impact.
- **Spiritual Discernment:**
- These strategies enhance spiritual discernment. The prophet, attuned to the Spirit, receives insights into hidden issues, enabling precise, Spirit-led prayers.
- **Alignment with God's Timing:**
- Prophetic prayer strategies operate in alignment with God's timing. Understanding the seasons and timing of God ensures that prayers are effective and usher in divine intervention at the appointed hour.
- **Aid in Spiritual Warfare:**
- Prophetic prayer strategies serve as potent weapons in spiritual warfare. By identifying and targeting strongholds, they contribute to the tearing down of the enemy's plans and fortifications.

Unveiling Kingdom Realities Through Prophetic Prayer:

In conclusion, prophetic prayer strategies are not a religious exercise but a dynamic journey into the heart of God's will. As prophets and believers alike engage in strategic, Spirit-led intercession, they unlock the gates of heaven, releasing transformative power into every sphere of influence.

May this chapter serve as a call to embrace the divine responsibility of prophetic prayer strategies. Let us journey together, armed with the Word, led by the Spirit, and fervently seeking the face of our Heavenly Father. In the realm of prophetic prayer, we become conduits for the miraculous, agents of transformation, and vessels through which God's Kingdom is established on earth as it is in heaven.

CHAPTER 6
Navigating Challenges in Prophetic Ministry

Navigating Challenges: A Prophet's Journey through Pitfalls and Victories:

In the multifaceted terrain of prophetic ministry, challenges and pitfalls are not just occasional companions; they are integral aspects of the prophetic journey. As we explore the common obstacles faced by prophets, both in my personal experiences and biblical narratives, it becomes evident that the path of a prophet is marked by both trials and triumphs.

Personal Encounter: Unveiling the Captive Atmosphere

Several years ago, I found myself invited to preach at a church eager to experience the prophetic. As I began to prophesy, an unexpected tension gripped the atmosphere. It was as if an invisible force sought to resist the flow of God's Spirit. I began to discern through the Holy Spirit that a religious spirit was sent from the satanic kingdom to bind the people to keep them from receiving the Prophetic Anointing. Discerning this opposition, I realized that a spiritual stronghold was holding the congregation captive.

In that challenging moment, I relied on the authority given by the Holy Spirit. With a boldness that can only come from divine assurance, I rebuked the spirit attempting to hinder the prophetic flow. As I spoke the words of rebuke, there was a palpable shift in the atmosphere. The captives were set free, and the prophetic utterances flowed with renewed freedom and power. People began to receive breakthroughs and healing took place. Miracles manifested in the building left and right. So many testimonies began to manifest as the people praised Jesus for revealing His love and power through the Prophetic grace.

Biblical Examples: Prophets Facing Challenges:
- **Elijah on Mount Carmel (1 Kings 18):**
- Elijah confronted the prophets of Baal in a dramatic showdown on Mount Carmel. Despite witnessing the miraculous display of God's power, Elijah soon found himself fleeing for his life from the threats of Queen Jezebel. In his exhaustion and fear, he faced the challenge of despondency and isolation. Lesson: Even after remarkable victories, prophets may encounter moments of emotional and spiritual vulnerability. God's response to Elijah's challenge was not just a rebuke but also a tender provision, highlighting the need for rest, nourishment, and divine encouragement.
- **Jeremiah's Loneliness and Rejection (Jeremiah 20):**
- Jeremiah, known as the weeping prophet, faced intense opposition and rejection. His message of impending judgment was met with hostility, leading to personal suffering and a sense of isolation. **Lesson:** Prophets often grapple with loneliness and rejection. Jeremiah's perseverance in

the face of adversity speaks to the resilience required in the prophetic calling.

Common Pitfalls in Prophetic Ministry:
- **Misunderstanding and Criticism:**
- Prophets may be misunderstood, and their messages can be met with criticism. This can lead to isolation and discouragement.
- **Spiritual Attacks and Warfare:**
- The enemy targets prophets with spiritual attacks to hinder their effectiveness. Prophetic voices may face opposition from both spiritual and human sources.
- **Balancing Humility and Authority:**
- Striking the right balance between humility and the authority inherent in the prophetic calling can be a challenge. Pride can undermine the authenticity of the prophetic message.
- **Navigating Timing and Patience:**
- Discerning the timing of prophetic words and patiently waiting for their fulfillment can be challenging. Impatience may lead to frustration and doubt.

Overcoming Pitfalls: Strategies for Victory:
- **Cultivate Humility and Teachability:**
- A humble heart and a teachable spirit are essential to navigate criticism and misunderstanding. Embrace correction and continue growing in your understanding of the prophetic.
- **Invest in Spiritual Discernment:**
- Develop a keen sense of spiritual discernment. Prophetic voices must distinguish between God's voice, their own desires, and external influences seeking to distort the message.

- **Embrace Spiritual Warfare:**
- Acknowledge the reality of spiritual warfare and be equipped with the armor of God (Ephesians 6:10-18). Prophets should actively engage in prayer, fasting, and spiritual warfare to overcome opposition.
- **Cultivate Patience and Trust in God's Timing:**
- Patiently await the fulfillment of prophetic words, trusting in God's perfect timing. Elijah's journey into the wilderness (1 Kings 19) teaches us that God provides sustenance for the prophetic journey.

The Journey Continues:

Let it be known that the challenges encountered by prophets are not roadblocks but stepping stones. The very nature of these challenges refines and shapes the prophet for greater effectiveness. With each victory over a pitfall, the prophetic voice emerges stronger, more resilient, and better attuned to the nuances of God's guidance.

May this exploration of challenges and victories in prophetic ministry serve as both a warning and an encouragement. As a prophet, you are not alone in your struggles. The same God who sustained Elijah, comforted Jeremiah, and empowered countless prophets throughout history is with you on this sacred journey. Embrace the challenges, for in overcoming them, you step into a greater manifestation of your prophetic calling. The journey continues, and the Author of your prophetic story is faithful to bring it to completion.

Rising from the Ashes: Overcoming Burnout and Discouragement in Prophetic Ministry:

The journey of a prophet is not a serene stroll along well-paved paths; it is a relentless trek through valleys of discouragement and times of being of burnt out. The weight of the prophetic mantle, coupled with the inevitable trials of ministry, can cast shadows on even the most resilient spirit.

The Shadows of Being Burntout: A Prophetic Reality:

The demands of prophetic ministry, with its incessant intercession, the weight of divine messages, and the burdens for the people, can create an environment ripe for burnout. Even the stalwart prophet Elijah, after his mighty victory on Mount Carmel, found himself in the throes of burnout, sitting under a juniper tree, longing for death (1 Kings 19:4).

Personal Reflection: When the Flame Flickers Low:

In the crucible of my own journey, there have been seasons when the flame of zeal flickered low. The burdens I carried for the flock, the weight of prophetic messages, and the emotional toll of intercession conspired to drain the well of spiritual vitality. It was during one such period that I found myself seeking solace under the juniper tree of weariness.

The discouragement deepened as individuals I had poured into, nurtured in the faith, and trained in the prophetic began to stray. Like Samuel with King Saul, I invested time, love, and spiritual guidance into their lives. Yet, some chose paths that led away from the divine calling of God. The betrayal cut deep, and the burnout intensified, but through prayer and fresh oil of anointing from the Holy Spirit, I found myself strengthened and renewed again.

Biblical Anchors: Prophets Navigating Discouragement:
- **Jeremiah, the Weeping Prophet (Jeremiah 20):**
- Jeremiah faced discouragement as his messages of impending judgment were met with hostility. The burden became so heavy that he expressed a desire to quit prophesying. Yet, he acknowledged that the word of the Lord was like a fire shut up in his bones, compelling him to continue. Lesson: Even in moments of discouragement, the prophetic calling is an indelible fire. It may flicker, but it cannot be extinguished.
- **Paul's Trials and Perseverance (2 Corinthians 4:8-9):**
- The apostle Paul faced various trials and challenges in his ministry, yet he persevered. He was struck down but not destroyed, perplexed but not in despair. Lesson: Perseverance in the face of trials is part of the prophetic journey. The power of God sustains even in moments of weakness.

Overcoming Burnout: Strategies for Resilience:
- **Seeking Solitude and Renewal:**
- Elijah found solace in the quiet whisper of God's voice on Mount Horeb (1 Kings 19:12). Prophets must retreat to the quiet places for renewal and restoration.
- **Surrounding Oneself with Support:**
- Elijah was not alone; he had Elisha by his side. Prophets need supportive communities, mentors, and companions in the journey.
- **Realigning with God's Perspective:**

- Jeremiah found resilience by realigning with God's perspective. Prophets must continually seek God's MIND to understand His purposes in the midst of discouragement.
- **Embracing the Sovereignty of God:**
- Paul's endurance stemmed from an understanding of God's sovereignty. Prophets, too, must surrender to the sovereign plans of God, trusting that He works all things for good (Romans 8:28).

Rising as Eagles from the Abyss:

In conclusion, the journey of overcoming burnout and discouragement is both personal and universal for prophets. The shadows may lengthen, and weariness may set in, but the prophetic mantle is designed to endure. The burnout becomes a refining fire, and the discouragement transforms into a call to deeper reliance on God.

I strongly pray that this chapter serves as a wellspring of encouragement for prophets navigating the valleys of weariness. As you rise from the ashes of burnout, may you soar as eagles, strengthened by the wind of the Spirit. Discouragement may visit, but it cannot build a permanent dwelling in the heart of a resilient prophet. The journey continues, and the One who calls you is faithful to renew your strength in His perfect time.

Embracing Setbacks: A Prophetic Path to Spiritual Growth:

In the realm of the prophetic, setbacks and missed marks are not signs of failure but stepping stones toward greater spiritual growth. The journey of a prophet is not a perfectly scripted narrative but a divine tapestry woven with the threads of victories and setbacks alike.

The Prophetic Path: Navigating Setbacks:

Setbacks are not detours on the prophetic journey; they are invaluable lessons waiting to be uncovered. Every missed mark, every moment of recalibration, is an opportunity for the prophet to draw closer to the heart of the One who orchestrates the symphony of revelation.

Biblical Examples: Prophets Learning from Setbacks:
- **Jonah's Detour (Jonah 1-4):**
- Jonah, called to prophesy against Nineveh, initially resisted and took a detour. His setback became a powerful lesson about God's mercy, compassion, and the futility of fleeing from the divine call. Lesson: Setbacks can be divine interventions, redirecting the prophet toward the heart of God's purposes.
- **Peter's Denial (Matthew 26:69-75):**
- Peter, a pillar among the disciples, faced a setback when he denied Jesus three times. Yet, this failure became a catalyst for Peter's humility and a deepening understanding of grace. Lesson: Setbacks humble the prophet, creating fertile ground for the seeds of grace and mercy to flourish.

The Prophetic Pruning: Learning from Missed Marks:
- **Humility Through Imperfection:**
- A prophet's journey is a continual process of humbling. Setbacks teach humility, reminding the prophet that the gift is divine, and any accuracy is a manifestation of God's grace. This is important. NEVER FORGET THAT!!
- **Seeking the Source:**

- Setbacks prompt prophets to seek the Source rather than relying solely on their gifting. The prophetic is not about performance but about being conduits for God's voice.
- **Refining Discernment:**
- Mistakes in the prophetic refine discernment. The process of learning from setbacks sharpens the prophet's ability to distinguish between their own thoughts and the voice of God.

Encouragement to Fellow Prophets: Fear Not the Setbacks:
- **Courage to Be Wrong:**
- The fear of being wrong stifles prophetic growth. Embrace the courage to miss the mark, knowing that even in setbacks, God's redemptive hand is at work.
- **Community and Accountability:**
- Create a community of accountability. A circle of fellow prophets and mentors provides a safe space to share setbacks, receive guidance, and collectively grow in the prophetic.
- **Perseverance in Prayer:**
- Persevere in prayer, seeking God's guidance not only for accuracy but also for the wisdom to navigate setbacks with grace and resilience.

Setbacks as Stepping Stones:

In conclusion, setbacks are not roadblocks but stepping stones. The prophet's journey is a progression toward spiritual maturity, and each missed mark contributes to the unfolding narrative of growth. The prophetic is not about perfection but about a relentless pursuit of the One who calls, corrects, and commissions.

May this chapter serve as a balm for the discouraged prophet, a reminder that setbacks are not indicators of inadequacy but opportunities for deeper communion with the Divine. Fear not the missed marks, for in each setback, God is shaping a more resilient, more compassionate, and more accurate prophet. The journey continues, and every setback is a testament to the unwavering faithfulness of the One who guides us through the prophetic odyssey.

CHAPTER 7

The Prophetic and Leadership

The Tightrope of Authority and Humility: A Prophet's Balancing Act:

In the intricate dance of prophetic leadership, the delicate balance between authority and humility is not just a desirable quality but an imperative for those called to guide God's people. The allure of authority, when not tethered to the anchor of humility, can lead to perilous heights of pride. In this chapter, we explore the prophet's perspective on maintaining equilibrium between authority and humility, drawing lessons from both scriptural insights and personal MY experiences.

The Authority of the Prophet: A Divine Mandate:

The prophetic mantle carries a weighty authority, a divine charge to speak on behalf of God and shepherd His people. However, this authority is not a license for self-elevation; it is a sacred trust that demands careful stewardship.

Biblical Anchors: Prophetic Authority and Humility:
- **Moses' Humility (Numbers 12:3):**
- "Now Moses was a very humble man, more humble than anyone else on the face of the earth." Moses, despite his unparalleled authority as a prophet, remained characterized by humility. Lesson: True prophetic authority is grounded in humility before God.
- **Paul's Thorn in the Flesh (2 Corinthians 12:7-10):**
- The apostle Paul, given visions and revelations, was humbled by a "thorn in the flesh." His weakness became a platform for God's strength. Lesson: Even in great authority, prophets are not exempt from weaknesses that foster humility.

Personal Reflection: Navigating Adoration and Bowing:

A FEW YEARS AGO, in a church service, I encountered a situation that illuminated the need for balance in prophetic authority. A well-meaning individual consistently bowed to the floor in reverence upon seeing me, expressing admiration for the prophetic ministry. While respect is honorable, the act of bowing crossed a critical line, blurring the distinction between honoring the prophetic gift and inadvertently elevating the vessel.

Addressing the Bowing Issue: A Lesson from Peter (Acts 10:25-26):

Just as Peter corrected Cornelius in Acts 10, I felt compelled to address the bowing issue. In humility, I shared that I was a fellow servant, not deserving of such reverence. I pointed to the truth that our worship is reserved for God alone. While appreciative of the respect, I emphasized the importance of directing adoration toward the Lord Jesus, not the and not me.

The Problem of Prophetic Elevation:
- **Erosion of Humility:**
- Constant adulation can erode the prophet's humility, fostering an inflated sense of self-importance.
- **Distorted Perceptions:**
- Excessive reverence can lead others to perceive the prophet as infallible, hindering a realistic understanding of human frailty.
- **Danger of Cult of Personality:**
- Unchecked adoration may inadvertently give rise to a cult of personality, diverting focus from God to the human vessel.

The Prophetic Balancing Act: Strategies for Maintaining Humility:
- **Accountability Partners:**
- Prophets should surround themselves with trusted individuals who can provide honest feedback and ensure humility is preserved.
- **Regular Self-Examination:**
- Regular introspection and self-examination help prophets guard against pride and maintain a humble posture before God.
- **Focusing on God's Glory:**
- Prophets must consistently redirect attention to God's glory. When the focus remains on Him, the risk of personal glorification diminishes.

The Sweet Spot of Authority and Humility:

In conclusion, the prophet's journey demands a delicate navigation between authority and humility. The authority bestowed upon prophets is not a pedestal for self-exaltation but a platform for God's glory. As prophets, let us walk humbly, mindful of our humanity, and resolute in directing all adoration toward the Almighty. The true sweet spot lies not in the elevation of the prophet but in the exaltation of the One who sends the prophetic word. May this chapter serve as a compass for prophets, guiding them in the sacred dance of authority and humility as they lead God's people with grace and integrity.

The Prophetic Navigator: Guiding the Body of Christ with Divine Direction:

In the intricate tapestry of the Body of Christ, the prophet emerges as a spiritual navigator, guiding and steering God's people through the currents of divine purpose. The prophet's role within the framework of the five-fold ministry is crucial, distinct, and vital for the edification and direction of the Church. This chapter explores the prophet's perspective on providing spiritual direction, emphasizing the stark differences between genuine prophetic ministry and secular practices like psychics and fortune-tellers.

The Prophetic Role in the Five-Fold Ministry:

The Apostle Paul, in Ephesians 4:11-13, outlines the five-fold ministry, and among these roles, the prophet stands as a unique conduit of divine guidance. The prophet is appointed to equip, edify, and unify the Body of Christ, serving as a spiritual compass pointing toward God's purpose.

Distinguishing the Prophet: A Divine Assignment:

Unlike psychics and fortune-tellers who operate from various belief systems, the prophet stands as a representative of the living God. The distinction lies in the source of their insight. Prophets receive divine revelations and speak forth messages given by God, rooted in biblical truth and aligned with the character of God.

Spiritual Direction: Guiding the Church on God's Path:
- **Revealing God's Heart:**
- Prophets are tasked with unveiling God's heart for His people. Through prayer, discernment, and revelation, they articulate the mind of God, providing insight into His desires, warnings, and promises.
- **Edifying and Correcting:**
- The prophet's ministry involves building up and correcting the Church. They bring encouragement and exhortation but are also entrusted with the responsibility of calling the Body to repentance and alignment with God's will.
- **Navigating Seasons and Strategies:**
- Prophets provide directional insight into the seasons and strategies ordained by God. Their role is to help the Church understand the timing and purpose of God's actions in the earth.

Differentiating Prophetic Ministry from Psychic Practices:
- **Source of Revelation:**
- Prophets receive revelations from the Holy Spirit and communicate messages from the divine, rooted in a relationship with the living God. Psychics, on the other hand, may draw from various spiritual beliefs or personal intuition.
- **Biblical Foundation:**
- The prophet's messages align with and build upon the biblical foundation. The authority of their words comes from scriptural truth, whereas psychics often operate outside of or contrary to biblical principles.
- **Motivation and Purpose:**

- Prophets are motivated by a love for God and His people, seeking their spiritual growth and alignment with God's will. Psychics may operate for personal gain or the satisfaction of human desires.

The Prophet's Caution: Guarding Against Misunderstandings:

Despite the noble calling, prophets must be vigilant against misunderstandings and misinterpretations. It's crucial to communicate that the prophetic is not a tool for personal fortune-telling but a ministry rooted in serving God's purposes and edifying His people.

Conclusion: Navigating with Divine Precision:

In conclusion, the prophet's role as a spiritual navigator within the Body of Christ is a sacred and weighty responsibility. Through divine direction, edification, and alignment with God's purposes, prophets contribute to the growth and unity of the Church. As the prophetic voice speaks, let it resonate with the echo of God's heart, guiding the Body with divine precision toward the fulfillment of His Kingdom purposes. May this chapter serve as a clarion call to honor and appreciate the vital role of prophets in steering the Church toward the path of righteousness and divine destiny.

Chapter 8

Recognizing False Prophets In A Sea of Voices

As a prophet, the responsibility extends beyond delivering divine messages—it includes discerning the authenticity of voices claiming prophetic authority. In the vast landscape of online platforms and social media, the contrast between true and false prophets becomes increasingly critical. This chapter explores the prophet's perspective on distinguishing between the genuine and the counterfeit, shedding light on the telltale signs of false prophets and recounting a personal encounter that underscores the importance of discernment.

The True Prophet's Mandate: A Divine Charge with Accountability:

True prophets, aware of the divine charge entrusted to them, understand that their role is not a pedestal for self-promotion or personal gain. Authentic prophetic ministry prioritizes the revelation of God's heart, the edification of the Church, and the fulfillment of God's purposes in the lives of His people.

Distinguishing Traits of False Prophets: A Prophet's Insight:
- **Prosperity-Centric Messages:**
- False prophets often center their messages on prosperity, abundance, and material gain, neglecting the deeper call to righteousness, holiness, and spiritual growth.
- **Financial Exploitation:**
- One glaring red flag is the exploitation of believers for financial gain. False prophets may manipulate individuals into paying for prophecies or sow seeds with the promise of immediate financial return.
- **Lack of Accountability and Correction:**
- Authentic prophets embrace accountability and correction. False prophets, however, may resist correction, viewing themselves as infallible and above scrutiny.
- **Absence of a God-Centered Message:**
- False prophets may accurately use spiritual gifts like the word of knowledge but miss the essence of a God-centered message. True prophetic words reveal God's plans, purpose, and calling for individuals beyond material blessings.

Personal Encounter: Discerning the Hollow Prophecy:

Let me share with you a time I was in a worship service; I witnessed a striking display of accurate word of knowledge that left the congregation in awe. The false prophet effortlessly called out specific names, birthdays, and even addressed personal struggles with uncanny precision. However, the unsettling reality unfolded when the prophecy unraveled, revealing a

focus solely on material blessings—cars, houses, and prosperity. There was a conspicuous absence of God's divine purpose and destiny for the individual's life. Then The Holy Spirit spoke to me and said THAT WAS NOT A PROPHECY! THAT WAS A PREFORMANCE! True Prophecy can include calling your name, address and birthday, but the meat of the message from God is either from these four frequencies:
1. Come To Jesus,
2. Stay With Jesus,
3. Do this for Jesus, and lastly
4. Go higher in JESUS. IF the prophecy is not filled with or coming from these four frequencies then it is not of God.

The Essence of True Prophecy: A Divine Blueprint for Purpose:

True prophecy, as exemplified in the biblical narrative, goes beyond the surface. It delves into the depth of God's purpose, calling individuals to repentance, righteousness, and a devoted relationship with the Creator. Authentic prophecy unveils the divine blueprint for a person's life, steering them toward their God-ordained destiny.

The Prophet's Call to Discernment: Protecting the Flock:
- **Grounded in Scripture:**
- A true prophet's discernment is anchored in the Word of God. Regular engagement with scripture fortifies discernment against false teachings.
- **Dependence on the Holy Spirit:**
- The Holy Spirit is the ultimate guide in discernment. Prophets must cultivate a deep reliance on the Holy Spirit for insight into the authenticity of spiritual messages.
- **Education and Awareness:**

- Prophets must educate themselves and others about the traits and tactics employed by false prophets. Awareness is a powerful shield against deception.

Guarding the Flock with Discernment:

In conclusion, the prophet's role extends beyond delivering messages; it includes safeguarding the flock from the deceptive allure of false prophets. Discernment, grounded in scripture and guided by the Holy Spirit, is the prophet's tool to distinguish between the genuine and the counterfeit. As the Body of Christ navigates the sea of voices, may discernment be a prevailing wind, steering believers away from the rocks of deception and into the safe harbor of God's truth. This chapter serves as a call to prophets and believers alike: guard your hearts, test the spirits, and embrace the discernment that safeguards the authenticity of God's prophetic word.

Discerning the Authentic: Navigating the Realm of True Prophecy:

In the intricate landscape of the prophetic, discernment is the compass that guides believers through the dynamic currents of authentic and counterfeit expressions.

"Beloved, do not believe every spirit, but test the spirits to see whether they are from God, for many false prophets have gone out into the world." (1 John 4:1)

Detecting a False Prophet: Warning Signs:
- **Contradiction to Scripture:**

- A false prophet's message contradicts the principles and teachings found in the Bible. God's Word is the ultimate standard against which all prophetic utterances must be measured.
- **Fruit Inspection:**
- Jesus taught that a tree is known by its fruit (Matthew 7:15-20). A false prophet's life will often exhibit inconsistencies, immorality, or a lack of spiritual maturity.
- **Focus on Material Gain:**
- False prophets may prioritize personal gain, using the prophetic gift as a means to financial exploitation. Authentic prophets seek to advance God's Kingdom, not their own prosperity.
- **Absence of Accountability:**
- True prophets willingly submit to spiritual authority and accountability. False prophets may resist correction and accountability, viewing themselves as above scrutiny.

Canceling False Prophecies: Empowering the Believer:

"But the prophet who presumes to speak a word in my name that I have not commanded him to speak, or who speaks in the name of other gods, that same prophet shall die." (Deuteronomy 18:20)

- **Prayer and Repentance:**
- Seek God in prayer, repenting for any areas where you might have unknowingly opened doors to false prophecies. Ask for His discernment and guidance.
- **Invoke the Authority of God's Word:**
- Declare God's Word over your life. Speak passages that align with His promises and refute any words spoken in contradiction.

- **Consult Trusted Spiritual Leaders:**
- Seek counsel from trustworthy spiritual leaders who can provide guidance, wisdom, and a biblical perspective on the prophetic words in question.
- **Renounce and Reject:**
- Verbalize your rejection of any false prophecies. Renounce them in the name of Jesus and declare His lordship over your life.

The True Prophetic Voice: A Guiding Light:

"When a prophet speaks in the name of the Lord, if the word does not come to pass or come true, that is a word that the Lord has not spoken; the prophet has spoken it presumptuously. You need not be afraid of him." (Deuteronomy 18:22)

In closing, be encouraged to embrace the authentic prophetic voices that align with God's truth. True prophets inspire confidence through their humility, adherence to scripture, and a genuine commitment to advancing God's Kingdom.

May this chapter serve as a guide, empowering you to discern the genuine from the counterfeit, and enabling you to cancel any false words spoken over your life. In the pursuit of the prophetic, let discernment be your constant companion, and may your journey be marked by the transformative power of true prophetic revelation.

CHAPTER 9

The Prophet's Cave: Solitude, Fasting, and Divine Encounter

In the journey of a prophet, there exists a sacred space—a metaphorical cave—that beckons them to a profound encounter with God. This chapter delves into the concept of the prophet's cave, a season of solitude and fasting that every prophet encounters. Within this spiritual cocoon, prophets are drawn into a deeper communion with the divine, purified for the reception of divine revelation.

The Cave: A Prophetic Sojourn into Solitude:

The prophet's cave is not a physical location but a spiritual realm—a season marked by isolation, fasting, and intensified prayer. It is a sacred space where the noise of the world fades, and the still, small voice of God becomes resoundingly clear.

Biblical Foundation: Prophetic Encounters in the Wilderness:
- **Moses on Mount Sinai (Exodus 34:28):**
- Moses, the great prophet, spent forty days and nights on Mount Sinai, fasting and communing with God. This solitude prepared him for receiving the divine law.
- **Elijah at Horeb (1 Kings 19:8):**
- Elijah, after a momentous victory and a season of exhaustion, found himself in a cave on Mount Horeb. In solitude, God spoke to him in a gentle whisper.

The Prophet's Isolation: Nurturing Spiritual Intimacy:
- **Purification Through Solitude:**
- The prophet's cave is a place of purification. In isolation, prophets shed the distractions of the world, allowing God to cleanse and refine their hearts.
- **The Refinement of Character:**
- Solitude refines the character of the prophet. It is in the quietness of the cave that God addresses any areas needing transformation or correction.
- **Intensified Prayer and Fasting:**
- Fasting becomes a powerful tool in the prophet's cave. Denying the physical sustenance intensifies spiritual sensitivity, creating an atmosphere conducive to divine revelation.

A Personal Sojourn: Forty Days of Fasting and Divine Presence:

In my own journey as a prophet, I experienced a profound sojourn in the prophet's cave—a season of forty days of fasting and prayer. The initial isolation felt daunting, but as the days unfolded, a palpable sense of God's presence enveloped me.

Divine Encounter in the Silence: A Prophetic Revelation:

In the stillness of the prophet's cave, God spoke in ways that transcended words. The divine encounters were not always filled with audible voices; rather, they were characterized by a deep sense of God's nearness, a profound knowing that surpassed human comprehension.

Revelation and Commissioning: The Fruit of Solitude:
- **Clarity of Vision:**
- The prophet's cave provides a clarified vision. In the solitude, the distractions dissipate, allowing prophets to see with spiritual acuity.
- **Divine Download of Revelation:**
- God, in His mercy, pours out revelations—insights into His plans, warnings for the future, and a deeper understanding of His character.
- **Commissioning for Service:**
- The prophet's cave is not merely a retreat; it is a training ground for the commissioning of divine assignments. Prophets emerge with a renewed sense of purpose and a zeal to fulfill God's mandates.

Emerging from the Cave Renewed:

In conclusion, the prophet's cave is not a detour but a divine destination. Every prophet encounters this sacred space, marked by solitude, fasting, and divine encounter. It is in the quietude of the cave that prophets are refined, purified, and commissioned for greater service. May this chapter serve as an invitation for prophets to embrace the sanctity of the cave, knowing that in the stillness, God's voice becomes unmistakably clear, and His revelations become a guiding light for the journey that lies ahead.

Chapter 10
Passing the Mantle: The Joy of Equipping Prophetic Voices

In the sacred tapestry of the prophetic, one of the noblest callings for a seasoned prophet is to impart, equip, and train the emerging generations in the prophetic ministry. I AM GOING TO UNVEIL the significance of passing the mantle, nurturing the growth of others in the prophetic, and rejoicing in the flourishing of diverse voices within the prophetic community.

Passing the Mantle: A Legacy of Prophetic Heritage:

Passing the mantle is not a mere tradition; it's a sacred act of imparting spiritual inheritance. In the Bible, Elijah passed his mantle to Elisha, signifying a transfer of authority and anointing. Similarly, contemporary prophets bear the responsibility to raise up successors, ensuring that the flame of the prophetic does not wane but intensifies with each generation.

Biblical Inspiration: The Multiplication of Prophetic Voices:
- Moses' Desire for a Prophetic Community (Numbers 11:29):
- Moses expressed a profound desire for all God's people to be prophets. The heart of a true prophet longs to see a proliferation of prophetic voices within the community of believers.
- Paul's Encouragement to Pursue Prophecy (1 Corinthians 14:1):
- The Apostle Paul urged believers to earnestly desire the gift of prophecy, emphasizing its edifying impact on the entire congregation.

The Joy of Equipping Others: Nurturing Prophetic Gifts:
- **Investing in the Next Generation:**
- Passing the mantle involves intentional investment in the lives of emerging prophets. This may include mentorship, impartation, and providing opportunities for practical prophetic exercises. In the next chapter, I will continue discussing the importance of prophets being mentored and shepherded.
- **Creating a Culture of Learning:**
- Establishing a culture of continuous learning is paramount. Workshops, teachings, and interactive sessions create an environment where prophetic gifts can be nurtured and refined.
- **Encouraging Risk-Taking:**
- To flourish in the prophetic, individuals must be encouraged to step out in faith. Mistakes are part of the learning process, and a safe environment fosters growth.

The Prophet's Joy: Seeing Others Flourish in the Prophetic:

Witnessing others blossom in the prophetic brings profound joy to the seasoned prophet. The genuine joy is not rooted in competition but in the understanding that the Kingdom of God is advanced as diverse prophetic voices contribute to the grand narrative.

Overcoming Intimidation: Embracing Diversity in the Prophetic:
- **Not Allowing Comparison to Stifle Growth:**
- The prophet must guard against the temptation of comparison. Each prophetic voice is unique, contributing a distinct piece to the BODY of CHRIST.
- **Motivation in Healthy Competition:**
- Rather than succumbing to intimidation, a seasoned prophet uses the excellence of others as motivation. Healthy competition fosters growth, propelling the prophet toward a deeper relationship with Christ.
- **Focusing on Jesus as the Source:**
- The ultimate focus remains on Jesus as the source of the prophetic. Every prophetic gift, regardless of its manifestation, finds its origin in Him.

Multiplying the Symphony of Voices:

Passing the mantle is not an act of relinquishing authority but a sacred stewardship of nurturing the prophetic landscape. I CAN NOT EXPRESS ENOUGH THE JOY I HAVE in seeing others rise, knowing that the multiplication of prophetic voices resonates with God's desire for a prophetic community. I PRAY THAT this chapter be an anthem for prophets to embrace the joy of equipping, to cultivate a culture of learning, and to celebrate the flourishing of diverse prophetic voices within the Body of Christ.

The Elijah-Elisha Dynamic: A Paradigm for Mentorship:

The relationship between Elijah and Elisha serves as an iconic illustration of mentorship in the biblical narrative. Elijah, a seasoned prophet, became a guiding light and mentor to Elisha, shaping and preparing him for a profound prophetic destiny.

Biblical Foundation: The Transfer of Anointing and Authority (2 Kings 2:9-15):

- **Elijah's Mantle:**
- Elijah, knowing his time on earth was drawing to a close, passed his mantle to Elisha, signifying the transfer of anointing and authority.
- **The Elisha Factor:**
- Elisha, in turn, received the mantle and went on to perform a double portion of miracles compared to Elijah. This exemplifies the exponential impact of effective mentorship.

The Prophetic Call to Mentorship: Nurturing the Next Generation:

- **Growth Through Shared Experience:**
- Mentorship provides a platform for shared experiences. Elijah and Elisha journeyed together, allowing the younger prophet to glean wisdom from the seasoned one.
- **Learning Through Observation:**
- Elisha observed Elijah's life, not just his prophetic actions. The nuances of character, perseverance, and dependence on God were vital aspects of the mentoring process.
- **The Importance of Corrective Guidance:**
- Mentorship includes correction. Elijah corrected Elisha when needed, fostering humility and a willingness to receive guidance.

The Accountability Umbrella: Why Every Prophet Needs a Mentor:
- **Avoiding Spiritual Drift:**
- A mentor acts as a spiritual anchor, preventing the protegé from drifting into uncharted or hazardous waters.
- **Navigating the Complexities of the Prophetic:**
- The prophetic journey is intricate, and a mentor provides invaluable guidance in navigating the complexities of hearing and delivering God's messages.
- **Preserving Humility in the Prophetic Gift:**
- Mentorship helps to anchor the prophet in humility. Accountability to a mentor curtails pride, ensuring the prophetic gift is wielded with grace and humility.

Personal Reflection: A Mentor's Impact on My Journey:

In my own journey as a prophet, I've been blessed to have a mentor who guided me through the ebbs and flows of the prophetic calling. Their wisdom, correction, and encouragement have been instrumental in shaping my character and refining my prophetic expression.

Overcoming the Fear of Accountability:
- **Understanding Accountability as a Shield:**
- Accountability is not a hindrance but a shield. A mentor provides a protective covering, ensuring the prophet stays aligned with God's purposes.
- **Seeing Correction as a Path to Growth:**

- Correction, though sometimes challenging, is a pathway to growth. A humble acceptance of correction fosters a deeper intimacy with God and refines the prophetic vessel.
- **Celebrating the Mentor's Success:**
- A true prophet does not fear the success of their mentor. Instead, they celebrate it as a testimony to the effectiveness of mentorship in raising powerful, anointed vessels for God's service.

The Tapestry of Mentorship in the Prophetic:

In conclusion, the tapestry of mentorship is intricately woven into the fabric of the prophetic journey. The Elijah-Elisha relationship serves as a timeless paradigm for the transformative power of mentorship. As prophets, let us embrace the wisdom, correction, and guidance that mentors provide. May this chapter be a catalyst for prophets to seek and value mentorship, recognizing its pivotal role in shaping, refining, and multiplying the impact of the prophetic gift within the Body of Christ.

CHAPTER 11

The Elijah-Elisha Dynamic: A Paradigm for Mentorship:

The relationship between Elijah and Elisha serves as an iconic illustration of mentorship in the biblical narrative. Elijah, a seasoned prophet, became a guiding light and mentor to Elisha, shaping and preparing him for a profound prophetic destiny.

Biblical Foundation: The Transfer of Anointing and Authority (2 Kings 2:9-15):
- **Elijah's Mantle:**
- Elijah, knowing his time on earth was drawing to a close, passed his mantle to Elisha, signifying the transfer of anointing and authority.
- **The Elisha Factor:**
- Elisha, in turn, received the mantle and went on to perform a double portion of miracles compared to Elijah. This exemplifies the exponential impact of effective mentorship.

The Prophetic Call to Mentorship: Nurturing the Next Generation:
- **Growth Through Shared Experience:**
- Mentorship provides a platform for shared experiences. Elijah and Elisha journeyed together, allowing the younger prophet to glean wisdom from the seasoned one.
- **Learning Through Observation:**
- Elisha observed Elijah's life, not just his prophetic actions. The nuances of character, perseverance, and dependence on God were vital aspects of the mentoring process.
- **The Importance of Corrective Guidance:**
- Mentorship includes correction. Elijah corrected Elisha when needed, fostering humility and a willingness to receive guidance.

The Accountability Umbrella: Why Every Prophet Needs a Mentor:
- **Avoiding Spiritual Drift:**
- A mentor acts as a spiritual anchor, preventing the protégé from drifting into uncharted or hazardous waters.
- **Navigating the Complexities of the Prophetic:**
- The prophetic journey is intricate, and a mentor provides invaluable guidance in navigating the complexities of hearing and delivering God's messages.
- **Preserving Humility in the Prophetic Gift:**
- Mentorship helps to anchor the prophet in humility. Accountability to a mentor curtails pride, ensuring the prophetic gift is wielded with grace and humility.

Personal Reflection: A Mentor's Impact on My Journey:
In my own journey as a prophet, I've been blessed to have several mentors mentor who guided me through the ebbs and flows of the prophetic calling. Their wisdom, correction, and encouragement have been instrumental in shaping my character and refining my prophetic expression.

Overcoming the Fear of Accountability:
- **Understanding Accountability as a Shield:**
- Accountability is not a hindrance but a shield. A mentor provides a protective covering, ensuring the prophet stays aligned with God's purposes.
- **Seeing Correction as a Path to Growth:**
- Correction, though sometimes challenging, is a pathway to growth. A humble acceptance of correction fosters a deeper intimacy with God and refines the prophetic vessel.
- **Celebrating the Mentor's Success:**
- A true prophet does not fear the success of their mentor. Instead, they celebrate it as a testimony to the effectiveness of mentorship in raising powerful, anointed vessels for God's service.

The Tapestry of Mentorship in the Prophetic:

In conclusion, the tapestry of mentorship is intricately woven into the fabric of the prophetic journey. The Elijah-Elisha relationship serves as a timeless paradigm for the transformative power of mentorship. As prophets, let us embrace the wisdom, correction, and guidance that mentors provide.

CHAPTER 12

Stepping into the Prophetic Destiny

As we conclude this journey through "The Making of a Prophet," I am filled with gratitude for the moments we've shared, the insights we've unearthed, and the divine encounters we've anticipated. This book is not merely a compilation of words but a roadmap guiding you toward a deeper walk with the Lord Jesus Christ.

Reflecting on the Journey:

In our exploration, we've delved into the intricacies of prophetic ministry, from understanding the call to navigating the challenges, embracing mentorship, and fostering a vibrant connection with our Lord Jesus. It is my sincere hope that the revelations imparted within these pages have been instrumental in shaping your understanding, stirring your hunger for righteousness, and propelling you into the fullness of your prophetic destiny.

"Now to Him who is able to do immeasurably more than all we ask or imagine, according to His power that is at work within us, to Him be glory in the church and in Christ Jesus throughout all generations, forever and ever. Amen." (Ephesians 3:20-21)

Let this scripture be an anthem resonating in the depths of your spirit—a declaration that the God we serve is not confined by our limitations or expectations. His power, at work within us, transcends our wildest dreams and imaginations. As prophets and believers, we stand on the precipice of immeasurable possibilities, guided by the sovereign hand of our Creator.

A Prophetic Prayer for Opened Eyes and Ears:

Dear Heavenly Father,

As we conclude this transformative journey, we stand on the cusp of a new season, filled with expectation and divine anticipation. Open the eyes of our understanding, Lord, that we may see the depths of Your truth. Unstop our spiritual ears, that we may hear the nuances of Your voice with clarity and precision.

Let a spirit of discernment rest upon us, distinguishing between the genuine and the counterfeit. May the revelations within this book become seeds planted in the fertile soil of our hearts, yielding a harvest of righteousness, love, and prophetic impact.

As we step into the fullness of our prophetic destiny, let the fragrance of Christ be evident in every word spoken, every action taken, and every life touched. May Your glory be manifest in and through us, drawing others into the transformative embrace of Your love.

In the name of Jesus, the Author and Finisher of our faith, we pray. Amen.

A Final Charge:

Beloved, may this closing chapter not mark the end but the beginning—a commencement into a realm of deeper revelation, heightened sensitivity to the Spirit, and a profound encounter with our Lord Jesus Christ. As you step into the fullness of your prophetic destiny, go with the assurance that He who called you is faithful to complete the good work He began in you. In the radiant love of Christ,

[PROPHET TIMOTHY LONG]

About The Author

"Before I formed thee in the belly I knew thee; and before thou camest forth out of the womb I sanctified thee, and I ordained thee a prophet unto the nations." Jeremiah 1:5 KJV

"Son of man, I have made thee a watchman unto the house of Israel: therefore hear the word at my mouth, and give them warning from me." Ezekiel 3:17 KJV

Prophet Timothy Long is a "Prophet of the Lord Jesus Christ".

Prophet Long is an anointed, Spirit-filled Prophet, Spiritual Father & Leader.
Prophet Long's ministry has grown to incorporate Covenant Partners, Sons & Daughters, and through the leading of the Holy Spirit, he now hosts weekly classes on understanding the Prophetic Mantle.

Prophet Long's mission and purpose are to show and prove God's mighty power through signs and wonders by the manifestation of powerful deliverances, healing, miracles, and prophecies.

His mission also includes preaching the Gospel: "The Word of Truth" with conviction, demonstration, and clarity.

Prophet Long's passion is to enable and encourage others to hear what the Spirit of God is saying, helping them also to be revived in their spirit, restored in their soul, transformed and renewed in their mind.

Prophet Long has studied for several years different teachings found in the scriptures, starting with:

Theology (Study of God),
Angelology (Study of Angels),
Christology (Study of Christ),
Pneumatology (Study of the Holy Ghost),
Soteriology (Study of Salvation),
and Eschatology (Study of the Last Days).

Studying the Word of God has enhanced Prophet Long's ability to flow into the prophetic with so much more accuracy, precision, and proven results. Thus ensuring that every prophecy he releases never contradicts scripture.

"In the beginning was the Word, and the Word was with God, and the Word was God." St. John 1:1 KJV

Prophet Timothy Long's Divine Assignment is to reveal the Mind and the Counsel of God to direct the church and to prepare them for the Second Coming of Jesus Christ.

Most importantly, edifying the body of Christ in all nations, and building the kingdom of God by winning souls, and being the Prophet, Preacher, Teacher that God has created him to be.

"The prophet that hath a dream, let him tell a dream; and he that hath my word, let him speak my word faithfully". Jeremiah 23:28 KJV

More Grace,

Prophet Timothy Long

Prophet Timothy Long

*For more information on upcoming events, register for classes, or to sow into the ministry, visit www.ProphetTimothyLongMinistries.com

Index

A

Abraham, 6, 8
abundance, 68
accountability, 59, 68, 71
achievement, 29
adversaries, 45
affirmation, 3, 10
anointing, 20, 56, 76, 79, 82
art, 22, 30, 32, 33, 38, 40
aspirations, 11
atmosphere, 26, 44, 49, 51, 52, 74
audible voices, 75
audience, 34
authority, 36, 39, 43, 47, 49, 52, 53, 61, 62, 63, 64, 65, 67, 71, 76, 78, 79, 82

B

background, 25
battle, 9, 45, 47
belief systems, 64
belly, 88
benchmark, 24
Bible, 13, 18, 37, 46, 71, 76
biblical principles, 65

blood, 10, 36, 45
Body of Christ, 5, 64, 66, 70, 78, 81
bones, 56
book, 13, 85, 86
breakthrough, 49
burnout, 55, 57

C

canvas, 34
captive, 45, 52
chains, 49
character, 1, 10, 14, 16, 17, 18, 19, 20, 21, 23, 65, 74, 75, 79, 80, 83, 84
clarion call, 66
clarity, 2, 15, 27, 32, 33, 86, 89
comfort, 11
commissions, 59
commitment, 3, 6, 28, 35, 37, 42, 72
communication, 23, 33, 35, 38, 39, 40
communion, 14, 22, 25, 60, 73
communities, 49, 56
community, 7, 10, 29, 42, 49, 59, 76, 77, 78
compass, 2, 4, 6, 11, 15, 28, 46, 64, 70
compassion, 2, 58
competition, 77, 78
confirmation, 24, 25, 26, 27, 30, 34
Cornelius, 62
cornerstone, 20, 22
correction, 2, 11, 27, 29, 40, 53, 68, 71, 74, 79, 80, 81, 83, 84
counterfeit, 67, 70, 72, 86
courage, 59
covenant, 3, 36
Creator, 1, 3, 11, 12, 23, 69, 86
cult, 63
culture, 11, 77, 78

D

darkness, 9, 44, 47
death, 55
deception, 47, 70
declarations, 49
desires, 17, 42, 43, 53, 65, 66
despair, 2, 9, 15, 49, 56
destination, 6, 27, 30, 75
detour, 58, 75
discern, 4, 23, 24, 25, 27, 33, 51, 72
discernment, 3, 23, 24, 25, 26, 28, 29, 30, 33, 46, 47, 49, 50, 53, 59, 65, 67, 69, 70, 71, 72, 86
discord, 45
discouragement, 45, 53, 55, 56, 57
distraction, 22
divine, 1, 2, 3, 4, 5, 6, 7, 8, 11, 13, 14, 15, 16, 17, 22, 24, 25, 27, 32, 33, 34, 35, 36, 37, 38, 39, 40, 41, 42, 43, 44, 45, 47, 48, 50, 52, 55, 57, 58, 61, 64, 65, 66, 67, 69, 73, 74, 75, 85, 86
Divine, 8, 11, 12, 14, 18, 22, 23, 25, 29, 32, 33, 37, 38, 39, 44, 60, 61, 64, 66, 67, 69, 73, 74, 75, 89
divine interventions, 58
divine presence, 7
doubts, 45
dreams, 8, 26, 30, 35, 86

E

eagle, 6, 7, 8, 36
earth, 41, 42, 44, 48, 50, 62, 65, 79, 82
earthquake, 25
edification, 64, 66, 68
Elijah, 25, 43, 46, 52, 54, 55, 56, 74, 76, 79, 81, 82, 83, 84
Elisha, 56, 76, 79, 81, 82, 83, 84
encounters, 6, 26, 30, 73, 75, 85
encouragement, 10, 52, 54, 57, 65, 80, 84
enemy, 10, 45, 47, 49, 50, 53
entitlement, 17

environment, 22, 55, 77
evil, 9, 28, 45
exhortation, 65
Ezekiel, 35, 36, 42, 88

F

failure, 27, 57, 58
faith, 3, 4, 6, 8, 19, 43, 45, 46, 55, 77, 87
faithful, 6, 10, 11, 17, 54, 57, 87
faithfulness, 3, 17, 19, 60
false prophets, 46, 67
false teachings, 69
fanfare, 4
fasting, 29, 46, 54, 73, 74, 75
Father, 6, 50, 86, 88
financial exploitation, 71
financial gain, 68
fingerprints, 5
fire, 7, 8, 25, 56, 57
flame, 55, 76
flames, 7
flesh, 10, 45, 62
flock, 55, 70
formula, 8
fortifications, 50
fortune-tellers, 64
foundation, 8, 9, 13, 15, 20, 65
frequencies, 4, 28, 29, 69
frequency, 22
fulfillment, 53, 54, 66, 68
full armor of God, 46

G

gates, 50
gentleness, 17, 19

glory, 3, 44, 47, 63, 86, 87
godliness, 16
gods, 71
goodness, 17, 19
Gospel, 89
grace, 12, 33, 34, 36, 40, 52, 58, 59, 64, 80, 83
guidance, 11, 16, 23, 27, 33, 37, 46, 54, 55, 59, 64, 71, 72, 79, 80, 81, 83, 84
gym, 7

H

hardships, 9, 42
healing, 52, 89
heart, 1, 4, 12, 13, 17, 18, 22, 25, 26, 29, 30, 31, 32, 37, 40, 42, 43, 50, 53, 57, 58, 65, 66, 67, 77
heartbeat, 1, 11, 42, 47
heaven, 9, 40, 42, 44, 48, 50
heavens, 7, 41
history, 2, 3, 54
holiness, 7, 36, 68
holy, 7
Holy Spirit, 29, 33, 34, 36, 37, 38, 39, 43, 47, 48, 51, 52, 56, 65, 69, 70, 88
homeland, 6
honor, 40, 66
hope, 15, 47, 85
hospitable, 17
hostility, 52, 56
humanity, 1, 11, 42, 63
humility, 5, 10, 20, 25, 26, 29, 30, 32, 34, 36, 37, 39, 40, 53, 58, 61, 62, 63, 64, 72, 79, 80, 83

I

identity, 9, 23, 43, 45
imagination, 4
immorality, 71

impartation, 77
impression, 23, 24
individuals, 2, 3, 6, 29, 41, 48, 55, 63, 68, 69, 77
influence, 20, 30, 50
inspiration, 3
instrument, 40, 44
intercession, 41, 42, 43, 44, 46, 48, 49, 50, 55
interpretations, 26, 35
intimidation, 78
isolation, 45, 52, 53, 73, 74
Israel, 36, 88
Israelites, 43

J

jargon, 34
Jeremiah, 36, 38, 52, 54, 56, 57, 88, 90
Jesus, 4, 6, 7, 8, 9, 22, 31, 47, 52, 58, 62, 69, 71, 72, 78, 85, 86, 87, 88, 89
Jonah, 58
Joseph, 35
journal, 30
journey, 4, 5, 6, 7, 8, 9, 10, 11, 14, 15, 16, 18, 22, 24, 25, 26, 27, 28, 29, 30, 31, 32, 35, 37, 38, 40, 42, 44, 49, 50, 51, 54, 55, 56, 57, 58, 59, 60, 63, 72, 73, 74, 75, 80, 81, 83, 84, 85, 86
joy, 17, 19, 20, 77, 78
judgment, 36, 52, 56

K

kindness, 17, 19, 20
King Saul, 55
kingdom of God, 2, 47, 90
Kingdom of God, 78
knowledge, 19, 45, 68

L

language, 23, 26, 34, 35, 37
leadership, 17
legacy, 9, 18, 20, 21
legalism, 45
lifestyle, 25, 31
loneliness, 52
Lord, 4, 7, 12, 16, 22, 25, 31, 35, 38, 47, 48, 56, 62, 72, 85, 86, 87, 88
lordship, 72
love, 1, 12, 17, 19, 20, 23, 34, 52, 55, 66, 86, 87

M

manifestation, 3, 7, 46, 47, 54, 58, 78, 89
mantle, 3, 11, 16, 17, 55, 57, 61, 76, 77, 78, 79, 82
Master Composer, 40
material gain, 68
maturation, 14
meditation, 14, 24, 25, 37
melody, 12, 20, 22
mentors, 25, 27, 30, 34, 56, 59, 81, 84
mentorship, 77, 79, 81, 82, 84, 85
mercy, 48, 58, 75
message, 24, 25, 26, 32, 33, 34, 36, 37, 39, 40, 45, 52, 53, 68, 69, 71
messages, 2, 4, 5, 23, 26, 32, 34, 35, 36, 44, 53, 55, 56, 65, 67, 68, 69, 70, 80, 83
metaphors, 35, 37
ministry, 16, 18, 19, 20, 21, 37, 41, 55, 56, 64, 65, 66, 88, 90
miraculous, 44, 50, 52
misinterpretations, 66
Mistakes, 26, 30, 59, 77
monologue, 38, 48
moral, 2, 16
Mount Carmel, 46, 52, 55
Mount Horeb, 56, 74
Mount Sinai, 74
mountains, 19
mouth, 38, 88

N

nations, 2, 41, 48, 49, 88, 90
nourishment, 52
nucleus, 41

O

obedience, 8
opposition, 8, 9, 44, 45, 46, 52, 53, 54
ordained, 8, 65, 69, 88
overseer, 17

P

paramount, 32, 77
passion, 41, 89
patience, 17, 19, 24
Paul, 9, 56, 57, 62, 64, 77
peace, 17, 19, 20, 42, 46
peers, 25, 27, 30, 34
persecution, 8, 9, 10
Perseverance, 10, 56, 59
Peter, 58, 62
pitfalls, 51
platform, 62, 63, 79, 83
power, 8, 18, 20, 43, 44, 45, 46, 47, 48, 49, 50, 52, 56, 72, 81, 84, 86, 89
prayer, 4, 10, 22, 24, 25, 26, 29, 30, 33, 34, 37, 41, 42, 43, 44, 46, 47, 48, 49, 50, 54, 55, 59, 65, 71, 73, 74
preach, 51
Preacher, 90
pride, 16, 17, 34, 61, 63, 80, 83
promises, 2, 3, 10, 15, 49, 65, 71
prophecy, 19, 28, 32, 35, 68, 69, 77, 89
prophet, 1, 2, 3, 7, 8, 9, 10, 11, 12, 13, 14, 15, 16, 17, 18, 19, 20, 21, 24, 25, 26, 28, 30, 32, 34, 35, 37, 38, 40, 41, 42, 43, 44, 45, 46, 47, 48, 50, 51, 52,

54, 55, 57, 58, 59, 60, 61, 62, 63, 64, 65, 66, 67, 68, 69, 70, 71, 72, 73, 74, 75, 76, 77, 78, 79, 80, 81, 82, 83, 84, 88, 90
prophet's cave, 73, 74, 75
Prophetic Anointing, 52
prophetic calling, 1, 3, 7, 13, 15, 18, 22, 53, 54, 56, 80, 84
prophetic destiny, 79, 82, 85, 86, 87
prophetic gift, 4, 6, 17, 62, 71, 78, 80, 81, 83
prophetic leadership, 7, 61
Prophetic Mantle, 88
prophetic ministry, 1, 2, 3, 4, 5, 6, 7, 8, 11, 13, 14, 15, 16, 17, 18, 19, 20, 28, 42, 48, 51, 54, 55, 62, 64, 67, 76, 85
Prophetic Ministry, 1, 16, 18, 51, 53, 55, 65
prophetic odyssey, 60
prophetic voice, 2, 9, 18, 47, 54, 66, 78
prophetic voices, 72, 77, 78
prophets, 2, 3, 5, 6, 9, 10, 11, 15, 30, 36, 46, 47, 50, 51, 52, 53, 54, 57, 59, 62, 63, 64, 66, 67, 68, 70, 71, 72, 73, 74, 75, 76, 77, 78, 81, 84, 86
Prophets, 2, 45, 47, 49, 52, 53, 54, 56, 57, 58, 59, 63, 64, 65, 66, 67, 68, 69, 70, 75
prosperity, 68, 69, 71
psychics, 64, 65
purity, 17, 34, 36
purpose, 1, 2, 3, 5, 11, 12, 64, 65, 68, 69, 75, 89

Q

Queen Jezebel, 52

R

recalibration, 58
red flag, 68
redemption, 3, 12, 43
rejection, 52, 72
relationship, 14, 27, 39, 65, 69, 78, 79, 81, 82, 84
religious spirit, 45, 51
repentance, 2, 65, 69

respectable, 17
reward, 9
righteousness, 2, 3, 42, 46, 66, 68, 69, 85, 86
roadblocks, 54, 59

S

salt, 33
salvation, 44, 46
Samuel, 55
satanic kingdom, 51
season, 34, 42, 49, 73, 74, 86
self-control, 17, 19
self-promotion, 67
self-reflection, 30
Setbacks, 57, 58, 59
shadows, 55, 57
sheep, 23
Shepherd, 23, 24
shield, 46, 70, 80, 84
sin, 3, 48
skill, 22, 31, 34, 35
social media, 67
solace, 2, 9, 11, 55, 56
soul, 4, 8, 11, 89
soundtrack, 27
spiritual acuity, 75
spiritual cocoon, 73
spiritual gifts, 18, 19, 28, 68
spiritual growth, 37, 57, 66, 68
spiritual maturity, 28, 59, 71
spiritual realm, 4, 27, 28, 73
spiritual revelation, 6
spiritual warfare, 9, 10, 44, 46, 47, 49, 50, 54
stewardship, 61, 78
storms, 10, 13, 20
strength, 5, 7, 8, 10, 13, 16, 36, 57, 62

strongholds, 45, 46, 47, 48, 49, 50
successors, 76
sword, 46, 49
symbolism, 26, 35
symbols, 35, 36, 37
symphony, 12, 20, 22, 25, 27, 28, 40, 58

T

tapestry, 1, 7, 8, 11, 18, 19, 35, 37, 40, 44, 48, 57, 64, 76, 81, 84
Teacher, 90
teachers, 26
teachings, 71, 77, 89
temperate, 17
temptation, 16, 78
testimonies, 52
tongues, 19, 28
transformation, 2, 3, 6, 44, 49, 50, 74
trials, 8, 51, 55, 56
triumphs, 51
trust, 34, 61
trustworthy, 17, 72
truth, 9, 13, 18, 23, 24, 33, 45, 46, 62, 65, 70, 72, 86

U

uniqueness, 5, 6
utterances, 2, 15, 39, 52, 71

V

valleys, 55, 57
vessel, 1, 4, 12, 32, 39, 40, 62, 63, 81, 84
victory, 45, 54, 55, 74
visibility, 17
vision, 1, 6, 7, 26, 36, 37, 75
visions, 8, 36, 62

Visions, 26

W

warnings, 2, 65, 75
watchman, 88
weakness, 5, 56, 62
weariness, 55, 57
whispers, 4, 11, 14, 25, 29, 37, 39
wife, 17
wisdom, 3, 13, 33, 38, 59, 72, 79, 80, 81, 83, 84
Workshops, 77
world, 14, 15, 22, 25, 41, 45, 70, 73, 74
worship service, 68

Z

zeal, 55, 75